THE REUNION

A Shocker by

Billy St. John

SAMUEL FRENCH, INC.
45 WEST 25TH STREET   NEW YORK 10010
7623 SUNSET BOULEVARD   HOLLYWOOD 90046
LONDON   TORONTO

Copyright © 1999, 2000 by Billy St. John

ALL RIGHTS RESERVED

CAUTION: Professionals and amateurs are hereby warned that THE REUNION is subject to a royalty. It is fully protected under the copyright laws of the United States of America, the British Commonwealth, including Canada, and all other countries of the Copyright Union. All rights, including professional, amateur, motion pictures, recitation, lecturing, public reading, radio broadcasting, television, and the rights of translation into foreign languages are strictly reserved. In its present form the play is dedicated to the reading public only.

The amateur live stage performance rights to THE REUNION are controlled exclusively by Samuel French, Inc. and royalty arrangements and licenses must be secured well in advance of presentation. PLEASE NOTE that amateur royalty fees are set upon application in accordance with your producing circumstances. When applying for a royalty quotation and license please give us the number of performances intended, dates of production, your seating capacity and admission fee. Royalties are payable one week before the opening performance of the play to Samuel French, Inc., at 45 W. 25th Street, New York, NY 10010; or at 7623 Sunset Blvd., Hollywood, CA 90046, or to Samuel French (Canada), Ltd., 100 Lombard Street, Toronto, Ontario, Canada M5C 1M3.

Royalty of the required amount must be paid whether the play is presented for charity or gain and whether or not admission is charged.

Stock royalty quoted on application to Samuel French, Inc.

For all other rights than those stipulated above, apply to Samuel French, Inc.

Particular emphasis is laid on the question of amateur or professional readings, permission and terms for which must be secured in writing from Samuel French, Inc.

Copying from this book in whole or in part is strictly forbidden by law, and the right of performance is not transferable.

Whenever the play is produced the following notice must appear on all programs, printing and advertising for the play: "Produced by special arrangement with Samuel French, Inc."

Due authorship credit must be given on all programs, printing and advertising for the play.

ISBN 0 573 62747 9   Printed in U.S.A.   #19952

No one shall commit or authorize any act or omission by which the copyright of, or the right to copyright, this play may be impaired.

No one shall make any changes in this play for the purpose of production.

Publication of this play does not imply availability for performance. Both amateurs and professionals considering a production are *strongly* advised in their own interests to apply to Samuel French, Inc., for written permission before starting rehearsals, advertis-

No part of this book may be reproduced, stored in a retrieval system, or transmitted in any form, by any means, now known or yet to be invented, including mechanical, electronic, photocopying, recording, videotaping, or otherwise, without the prior written

IMPORTANT BILLING AND CREDIT REQUIREMENTS

All producers of THE REUNION *must* ve credit to the Author of the Play in all programs distributed in connection with performances of the Play and in all instances in which the title of the Play appears for purposes of advertising, publicizing or otherwise exploiting the Play and/or a production. The name of the Author *must* also appear on a separate line, on which no other name appears, immediately following the title, and *must* appear in size of type not less than fifty percent the size of the title type.

CHARACTERS

MARY BETH CLARK-DAWSON, former high school student body secretary

JULIA JAMISON, former high school student body valedictorian

DR. TIM GRANT, former high school student body vice-president

SUZANNE BRINKERHOFF, former high school student body treasurer

ALEX DAWSON, former high school student body president

WILTON HACKETT, a classmate

CALLIE MORRIS, Julia's employee

The voices of
FEMALE TV ANCHOR
MALE TV ANCHOR (AL)
TV FIELD REPORTER (KIMBERLY TATE)
POLICE DETECTIVE LT. JOHN LAWTON

SYNOPSIS OF SCENES

TIME: The Present.
PLACE: Julia Jamison's apartment
atop a downtown office building in
Cleveland, Ohio.

ACT I: Scene 1 -- December 18. Thursday. 7:30 p.m.
Scene 2 -- December 19. Friday. 6:40 p.m.
Scene 3 -- Later that night. 10:55 p.m.

INTERMISSION

ACT II: Scene 1 -- Immediately following.
Scene 2 -- December 20. Saturday. 1:20 a.m.

ACT I

Scene 1

(December 18. Thursday. 7:30 p.m.
The setting is a loft apartment on the fourth and top floor of an office building in downtown Cleveland, Ohio. It belongs to the owner of the building, JULIA JAMISON, whose advertising agency occupies the lower floors. She uses the apartment as a pied à terre, *staying here most week nights rather than drive to her home on Lake Erie several miles out of town where she spends her weekends. The building is old, but Julia has obviously spent a lot of money refurbishing it. It has high ceilings. There are no windows; we might assume they occupy the fourth wall, though no reference is made to them.*
There is a set of elevator doors SR of the US wall. An old-fashioned dial is over the doors, one that has an arrow which moves to indicate at which of the four floors the elevator is at any given time. A brass plate and single button are beside the doors. A light switch is on the wall SR of the doors. When the doors are open, we see the interior of an elevator beyond them, dimly lighted from above. One of its walls is hinged to provide access to and from the elevator when the doors are closed.
A coat rack stands in the UR corner of the room, SR of the elevator; Julia's coat is on it. A floor lamp with a low-wattage bulb is SL of the doors. Spanning the center of the US wall, inset from the main room, is a kitchenette area: there is a counter with a sink at the middle. Under the SR counter is a short, apartment-size refrigerator. Inside it is a cake, carton of half-and-half, and other items. There are two drawers under the SL counter, and under them, a cabinet door behind which is a trash container. There is a large cabinet mounted over each counter; each has a door behind which are three shelves. A coffee maker, butcher block of knives, a dish towel, a roll of paper towels, a liquid soap dis-

penser, and a glass sit on the SR counter; the coffee maker is plugged into an electrical outlet [live] on the wall above the SR counter. On the shelves of the SR unit are a sugar bowl and creamer as well as food items such as snacks, soups, etc. On the shelves of the SL unit are glasses, cups, saucers, plates, bowls for microwaving foods, etc. A wooden chopping board and a microwave sit on the counter under this unit. A narrow, single-shelf cabinet with two doors is above the sink, joining the two large cabinets together; inside are a can of coffee and a package of coffee filters. A light with a florescent tube is mounted under it. Its switch is on the wall under the cabinet SR, along with a switch to the garbage disposal.

A few feet DS of the sink and cabinets is a serving bar which is open at the back. A wall angles from the kitchen area to the SL corner of the room. A door in this wall opens to a small bath. A sink is visible when the door is open. A liquid soap dispenser is beside it. There is a door in the SL wall that opens out to a bedroom; a light switch is on the wall beside the doorway. A computer desk is at the DR corner of the room. On it is a computer whose screen faces US, as well as a printer, floppy disk file, cordless telephone, manuals, a pad and pencil, etc., and a business envelope with checks inside. Inside a desk drawer are two paperclipped stacks of paper, one thick and one thin. Above the unit is a modern desk chair on casters. A light hangs above the desk from a chain.

A credenza spans the middle of the SR wall; a small, artificial Christmas tree is set at its center. Attractive pictures are hung above the unit and on the walls SL. A round table with four chairs is DC, DS of the serving bar. A television sits on a stand in the DL corner of the room, angled with its screen facing UR. A comfortable looking recliner which can swivel is in front of the television. A rolling cart, which is usually put against the wall US of the tv, is now DL. A television remote and a slide projector sit on it; a VCR unit is on its lower shelf. The projector is plugged into an outlet [live] on the wall behind the television; it is aimed at the bathroom door. The room reflects wealth and taste, a pleasing mixture of the old architecture and modern furnishings.

THE REUNION

AT RISE: The stage is empty. After a beat, we hear the SOUND of an ELEVATOR MOTOR RUNNING. The floor indicator dial over the elevator will move from 1 to 4. The SOUND stops and there is a DING. The doors slide open to reveal MARY BETH CLARK-DAWSON. MARY BETH is about 28 years old, as are the other members of the reunion committee. She is a plump, pretty woman — especially plump at the moment because she is seven and a half months pregnant. She is good-natured and friendly. She wears a coat over a maternity outfit — perhaps a jumper over a blouse or knit sweater — and has a purse on a strap over her shoulder. She holds a card key in one hand, and a shopping bag with a scrapbook and an address book inside in the other. She enters hesitantly and looks around; obviously, she hasn't been in the room before now.)

MARY BETH. Julia?

(The elevator doors slide shut behind her, making her jump.)

JULIA. *(Off SL.)* Mary Beth? I'll be right there. Come on in.

(MARY BETH takes a couple of steps DS, looking around as she puts the card key into her purse.)

MARY BETH. Oh, this is nice ... this is really nice.

(JULIA JAMISON enters SL, carrying several hand towels. JULIA is a beautiful, smart, sophisticated woman who was her class prom queen ten years ago. She is also well off financially, owning the office building and the ad agency it houses. She wears a blouse and a suit skirt without the jacket. When MARY BETH sees JULIA, she SQUEALS. JULIA hesitates a beat as if undecided whether to respond in kind, then, figuring "what the hell?", she SQUEALS back. JULIA lays the towels on the bar and crosses to MARY BETH. They hug.)

JULIA. Just look at you!

MARY BETH. Please, don't! I look a fright! You, on the other hand, look every bit as beautiful as you did the night you were crowned prom queen. I hate you!

JULIA. No, you don't.

MARY BETH. Yes, I do! But then, I hate every woman who can still see her feet.

JULIA. *(Laughing.)* Let me take your coat.

(MARY BETH puts her purse and shopping bag on the credenza. JULIA helps her off with her coat and hangs it on the rack in the UR corner.)

MARY BETH. I love your apartment.

JULIA. Thanks. When I bought the office building, I decided to use the lower floors for the ad agency, and fix the top one up as a *pied à terre* to stay in during the week. On weekends, I drive out to my home at Bay Village. It's on Lake Erie.

MARY BETH. Oooohhh ... right on the lake.... I bet it's nice, too.

JULIA. I like it. You and Alex will have to come out sometime. Maybe next summer.

MARY BETH. That sounds wonderful. I only hope I'll be able to get back into a bathing suit by then.

JULIA. Alex said the baby's due in six weeks. The end of January till ... oh, maybe July ... will give you plenty of time.

MARY BETH. That's easy for you to say.

JULIA. I guess I'd better start the coffee. I had a client stay past closing, so I'm running a little late. Come talk to me.

(They cross to the kitchen area.)

MARY BETH. Can I help?

JULIA. You could put those hand towels by the bathroom sink. Right around the corner

(MARY BETH picks up the towels and enters the bath where she'll put them on the sink.)

THE REUNION

MARY BETH. This is handy. Good. A pregnant lady always needs to know where the nearest bathroom is.

(She re-enters as JULIA opens the SL door to the short cabinet over the sink. She'll take a can of coffee and package of filters from there, set them on the counter, flip the switch on the wall under the SR cabinet which turns on the florescent light over the sink, and begin to fill the coffee pot from the coffee maker on the counter with water. She will proceed to pour the water into the coffee maker, put coffee into a filter using a measuring cup inside the can, put it in the machine, and turn on the unit which will actually make coffee. She will then replace the coffee can and package of filters in the cabinet and close the door.)

JULIA. I'm sorry you missed the organizational meeting last month. Alex said you weren't feeling well.

MARY BETH. It's his fault. Every ache, pain and bout of nausea I've had for the last seven months is his fault ... *(patting her stomach)* ... if you know what I mean.

JULIA. I'll take your word for it. Where is Alex?

MARY BETH. All of the school system's football coaches are meeting to plan next spring's awards banquet. Don't ask me why they decided they had to meet the week before Christmas when everything is so hectic, but they did. Men!

JULIA. I suspect most coaches' main religion is sports, anyway.

MARY BETH. I can't argue with that. Anyway, Alex said he'll get here as soon as he can.

JULIA. He gave you one card key and kept one for himself?

MARY BETH. Yep. I saw him put it in his wallet.

JULIA. Fine. Then he can let himself in the front door and take the elevator up, like you did.

MARY BETH. You aren't afraid somebody could get a hold of one of your cards and break in?

JULIA. I'm very careful who I give them to, and there's nothing on them to indicate what they go to. Besides, if I ever need to, I can change the combination in the door lock and the elevator by punching in a new one on the key pads.

MARY BETH. That's good to know.

JULIA. As for you guys, I certainly trust everyone on our committee. If you haven't become notorious criminals since high school, I figure none of you will slink in during the night and murder me in my bed.

(During the following, she will open the door to the SR cabinet, take out a sugar bowl and creamer, set them on the counter, close the cabinet door, open the refrigerator, take out a small carton of half-and-half, and pour some into the creamer.)

MARY BETH. You're giving me the shivers. What else can I do?

JULIA. You can get the cups and saucers from the other cabinet. *(MARY BETH opens the door of the SL cabinet, takes 5 cups and saucers from a shelf, puts them on the bar, and closes the door.)* There are spoons in the end drawer.

(MARY BETH will take 5 spoons from the end drawer and put them on the bar.

The ELEVATOR MOTOR starts. The elevator will descend to the first floor, pause, then ascend back to the fourth. The dial will indicate this.)

MARY BETH. Done.

JULIA. Napkins are in the next drawer.

(MARY BETH opens the drawer beside the first one, takes out 5 cloth napkins, shuts it, and puts the napkins on the bar.)

MARY BETH. *(Meaning the napkins.)* Pretty.

JULIA. I'll set out the dessert plates and forks when we take a break. *(She returns the half-and-half to the refrigerator.)* I'd better take this out now. *(She takes out a Sara Lee chocolate cake still in the box. She puts it on the bar.)* If I remember correctly, you like chocolate cake.

MARY BETH. *(Giggling.)* You should remember — you gave me your dessert every day through all four years of high school! That's why you look the way you do, and I look like this!

THE REUNION 11

JULIA. I thought Alex made you look like that?

(She takes a butcher knife from the block on the counter and puts it on the bar by the cake.)

MARY BETH. To be honest, I can blame him for the stomach — the rest of me is all my own doing.

JULIA. I think you look nice.

MARY BETH. Well, you can afford to be magnanimous — you haven't changed a bit. You're still gorgeous.

JULIA. *(Laughing.)* I knew there was some reason I liked you.

MARY BETH. Isn't it awful we haven't stayed in touch? I mean, we've both lived right here in the same city, and it took this reunion to get us back together.

JULIA. Ten years.... Where did the time go?

MARY BETH. I don't know about you, but mine went right to my hips.

(JULIA laughs. There is a DING and the elevator doors slide open. DR. TIM GRANT is there. TIM is a pleasant-looking man, a young physician. He wears brand-name pants and a nice shirt or sweater under his leather coat, preppy-looking and expensive in an understated way. He is obviously successful. A beeper is clipped to his belt.)

TIM. *(Entering.)* Anybody home?
JULIA. Over here.
MARY BETH. Tim?
TIM. In person.
MARY BETH. *(Rushing around the bar.)* Tim! Tim Grant! *(She SQUEALS.)*
TIM. Mary Beth Clark ... I mean, Clark-Dawson... *(Looking at her stomach.)* ... and company! Give me a hug!

(She rushes to him. They hug.)

MARY BETH. Oh, Tim, it's so good to see you!

THE REUNION

TIM. It's good to see you, too...both of you! Well, I don't have to ask what you've been doing lately.

MARY BETH. *(Giggling.)* Oh, you! ... and it wasn't lately! I don't mean we haven't ... *(Flustered.)* ... I mean ... oh, I don't know what I mean!

(TIM laughs, then removes his coat and hangs it on the rack.)

TIM. Actually, I knew you were pregnant. Alex told us all about it at our organizational meeting last month. Talk about a proud papa-to-be. Your first baby ... you must be excited.

MARY BETH. We really are, despite my complaining about the dubious joys of motherhood. We tried for five years, and then ... well ... it finally happened.

TIM. As Coach Biggers used to tell us on the basketball court: "Practice makes perfect!" Apparently, he was right.

(MARY BETH giggles. JULIA puts the sugar bowl and creamer on the bar and comes around it.)

JULIA. Hi, Tim.

TIM. Hi, beautiful. *(He crosses to JULIA. They hug.)* I'm on call at the hospital, but, miraculously, all my patients survived their surgeries today, so hopefully they'll lie quietly in ICU and not pop any stitches.

MARY BETH. *(Joining them.)* I can't believe you're a doctor, Tim.

TIM. Finally. Four years of college, then four of medical school, including a residency at Lutheran Hospital.... I've had my own practice a little over a year. If anyone at the reunion asks me what I've been doing since graduation, the answer is simple: I've been working my ass off.

JULIA. And such a cute ass. We cheerleaders used to get our jollies watching you dribble down the court in those tight silk shorts, didn't we, Mary Beth?

MARY BETH. We sure did. When we voted on the senior superlatives, the entire cheerleading squad wrote in "Best Butt — Tim

THE REUNION

Grant" on our ballots.

TIM. Oh, come on ...

JULIA. It's true. The yearbook sponsor ... what was her name? Miss Cunningham ... had a fit and threw our votes out.

MARY BETH. She was a sour old prune. Let's not invite her to the reunion.

JULIA. Too late — I've already sent the faculty their invitations. For what it's worth, Tim, if they had given a superlative for best ass, you would have gotten it.

TIM. Now you tell me. Just make sure you tell Eleanor when you meet her at the dinner-dance.

MARY BETH. Eleanor? Your wife?

TIM. Fiancée. She's a legal secretary. She works at the same law firm as my brother.

MARY BETH. I'm thrilled for you, Tim. I wish you every happiness.

TIM. Thanks. I figured it's time to take the plunge. Besides, patients like their doctors to be married. It seems to give us an air of respectability, for some strange reason — don't ask me why.

MARY BETH. Well, I look forward to meeting Eleanor.

JULIA. Me, too. I can't wait to fill her in on what ol' Tim, here, was like in high school.

TIM. If you do, you'd better hope you never need surgery and get me for your doctor. Come to think of it, I've got a few stories I could tell about you at the reunion, too. I wonder if Lydia Thomas ever found out who started the rumor she was turning tricks in the alley behind the Save-A-Lot on weekends?

JULIA. Enough said. Truce?

TIM. Truce.

(They shake hands.)

MARY BETH. You mean she wasn't?

(The ELEVATOR MOTOR starts. The elevator will descend to the first floor, pause, then ascend to the fourth again. The dial will indicate this.)

THE REUNION

TIM. Oh, I think she probably was — but not on a regular basis. Sounds like someone else has arrived. Alex?

MARY BETH. No, he'll be here a little later.

JULIA. That leaves Suzanne.

TIM. Suzie, the floozie — the original good time that was had by all.

MARY BETH. Oh, Tim!

TIM. Don't get me wrong, I like Suzanne, but the only difference between her and Lydia Thomas was Lydia charged for her favors, and Suzanne gave hers away for free.

JULIA. You want to repeat that to her face?

TIM. Are you nuts? I just put in twelve hours at a hospital and have no desire to go back to one tonight.

JULIA. Coward.

TIM. You got it. Be nice to me and I'll let you see the yellow stripe down my back.

JULIA. It's a tempting offer, but I'll pass. Eleanor might not like it.

TIM. Eleanor definitely would not like it. Um ... will you two ladies excuse me? I need to wash my hands. It's something doctors do a lot — I think it's called the "Lady Macbeth Syndrome."

JULIA. *(Gesturing to the bathroom.)* Help yourself.

(TIM crosses to the bathroom and exits, closing the door.)

MARY BETH. I love listening to you two kid around with each other. It's just like we were back in high school.

JULIA. Perish the thought.

(There is a DING and the elevator doors slide open to reveal SUZANNE BRINKERHOFF. SUZANNE is an attractive woman who is jaded, tough and extremely aggressive. She wears a chic, sexy cocktail dress. Her coat is draped over her arm and she carries an evening bag. She ENTERS, charging out of the elevator, and tosses the coat and purse onto the credenza. JULIA takes a couple of steps SR.)

JULIA. Hi, Suzanne.

THE REUNION

SUZANNE. Julia.

(She continues to charge DS. When MARY BETH sees her, she SQUEALS. SUZANNE stops in her tracks, startled.)

MARY BETH. Suzanne Brinkerhoff!
SUZANNE. *(A mumble.)* Mary Beth ... *(She charges SL, passing MARY BETH who expected a hug.)* Gotta pee.... *(She opens the bathroom door, rushes in, and stops, looking off SR of the doorway. We hear LIQUID SPLASHING INTO THE TOILET BOWL.)* Well, hel-lo, Tim! You're looking good!
TIM. *(Off SR of the door.)* Suzanne! Get out of here!
SUZANNE. *(Still staring at him.)* It's not as if I haven't seen it before.
TIM. *(Off.)* Suzanne!
SUZANNE. Oh, all right, but hurry up. You're not the only one who's got a bucket-load to empty.

(She steps back into the room and closes the door. JULIA grins, then crosses to UR, takes Suzanne's coat from the credenza, and hangs it on the coat rack.)

MARY BETH. Suzanne, Tim's engaged to be married!
SUZANNE. I heard. Lucky girl.
MARY BETH. Aren't you just thrilled to death for him?
SUZANNE. I can hardly stand it. *(Raising her voice.)* Tim! Any day now! *(Back to MARY BETH.)* So, Mary Beth ... Alex told us you were knocked up. How's the little mother?
MARY BETH. I've gained twenty pounds, my feet swell, my back aches, I sit on my pot more than my chairs, and I'm miserable twenty-four hours a day. Other than that, I'm fine.
SUZANNE. Better you than me, babe. *(She bangs on the bathroom door.)* Tim! I just had three margaritas at La Casa Verde's happy hour, and I'm about to do a Mexican hat dance!
MARY BETH. You don't have any children?
SUZANNE. Well, I was married to an overgrown kid a couple of years, but I got rid of him.

MARY BETH. You mean you got divorced?

SUZANNE. It was either that or stuff him down the garbage disposal. In retrospect, I realize that wouldn't have been nearly as messy as divorce court.

MARY BETH. I'm sorry it didn't work out. Suzanne, I have to tell you, that is a fabulous dress!

SUZANNE. Thanks. I have a late date. *(She bangs on the door.)* My God, man, I'm wearing pantyhose! Would you shake it off and let someone else have a turn!?!

(There is the SOUND OF A TOILET FLUSHING. TIM opens the door. He is drying his hands on a towel.)

TIM. It's all yours. I'm referring to the bathroom.

(He lays the towel on the sink and sweeps his arm in a "come in" gesture.)

SUZANNE. About time!

(She exits, rushing into the bathroom. TIM enters, coming into the room. She slams the door shut.)

TIM. *(To MARY BETH.)* Gee, that was embarrassing.

(JULIA crosses to them.)

JULIA. Well, you know Suzanne.

MARY BETH. It sounds as if you two know each other very well.

TIM. What can I say? When we were in high school, it was considered a rite of passage among the boys to sleep with Suzanne. To be accepted, you had to go to bed with her, whether you wanted to or not.

MARY BETH. Is that so? I wonder if Alex ...

TIM. *(Cutting in.)* Oh, honey, do yourself a favor — don't ask! Look, all that was a long time ago. Till the meeting last month, Suzanne and I hadn't seen each other since graduation.

THE REUNION

JULIA. I'd say you just made up for lost time. I can't wait for you to introduce Suzanne to Eleanor.

TIM. Oh, God! I'm not sure this reunion was such a good idea. I might cancel out.

MARY BETH. It was a great idea, and you have to be there! All of us on the committee have to be there. We were the student body officers.

JULIA. Tim is in charge of the door prizes, so he'll have to attend. Now that that's settled, I have an announcement to make: I think the coffee's ready.

(They cross to above the bar.)

TIM. Pour a big cup for Suzanne. Three margaritas? She needs it!

(They will take cups from the bar, get coffee from the pot, and add sugar and creamer at the bar.)

MARY BETH. How are the responses to the invitations coming in, Julia?

JULIA. Great. I'll show you. *(After she gets her coffee, she will cross to the computer desk, DR, sit, and turn on the computer. She will use the mouse to call up a file. TIM and MARY BETH will carry their cups and follow her, looking over her shoulder.)* I had Callie, the computer genius in my graphics department, build a file with all the graduates of ____ *(the date ten years ago)* listed in alphabetical order, including their addresses, e-mail addresses if they're on-line, and phone numbers. There's a column to indicate if they're coming to the reunion or not, and if they've sent their checks. Most of them have, since it's only two weeks away.

MARY BETH. For the dinner dance? Food, entertainment ...?

JULIA. Yeah, and a little extra to cover the teachers' dinners and incidentals such as postage. It's not all that much -- over half of the classmates are on-line, so I sent their invitations by computer. The rest, I mailed.

MARY BETH. *(Looking at the screen.)* Oh, you've listed their occupations, marital status, number of kids ...

JULIA. Didn't Alex tell you? We thought it would be a neat idea to print some little booklets with the students' — well, former students' — bios to hand out at the reunion. Catch everybody up. And we can mail copies to the ones who can't attend.

MARY BETH. I like it. I have to admit, when Alex told me you guys decided to hold the reunion on January third, I wondered if that's a good time of the year to have it. From what you say, I guess it is.

TIM. We discussed holding it around July the fourth, figuring that's a time lots of folks who have moved away could take their summer vacations, then Julia noticed that January third is on a Saturday this year.

(There is the SOUND of a TOILET FLUSHING.)

JULIA. A lot of out-of-towners I've kept in touch with come in around the Christmas holidays to be with their families. I thought most them might make plans to stay through New Year's and the reunion. Apparently, I was right; about seventy per cent of the class have confirmed so far. See? I'll scroll down the list. *(She does so.)*

TIM. Of course, there are some who wouldn't come, even if they lived right across the street from the school. *(Looking at the screen.)* Jim Adams ... wonder if his chronic jock itch ever cleared up?

MARY BETH. Ellen Batey Simpson? So Ellen finally got a husband after all...

(SUZANNE opens the bathroom door. She is wiping her hands on a towel.)

JULIA. Lester Buckner — yes ...
SUZANNE. Pee Wee Buckner? What about him?
MARY BETH. He's coming to the reunion. He's not that short — how did he ever get a nickname like Pee Wee?
SUZANNE. I gave it to him.

(She tosses the towel onto the sink and enters the room.)

MARY BETH. Never mind.

THE REUNION

SUZANNE. Still single?
MARY BETH. Yes.

(She supports her stomach with one hand as she leans over to look at the screen.)

SUZANNE. It figures.
JULIA. *(Rising.)* What am I thinking of ...? Here, Mary Beth, sit down.
TIM. Yeah — take a load off your feet.
MARY BETH. If you think that's a joke, it's not.

(She sits.)

JULIA. Use the mouse to pull the little bar down.
MARY BETH. Oh, I'm computer semi-literate. I use ours at home to store recipes and keep up with our household accounts, and I've even mastered e-mail.
SUZANNE. I'm impressed. Get with me later and I'll give you the addresses of some pretty spicy web sites.
TIM. Why does that not surprise me?
JULIA. I poured you some coffee, Suzanne. It's on the bar.
SUZANNE. Thanks.

(She takes her coffee and sips some.)

TIM. *(Still looking at the screen.)* Richard Eddington is bringing a "companion." I wonder if it's a male or female?
SUZANNE. I wonder if it's a human.
JULIA. There are still twenty or so classmates we haven't been able to locate, and we're getting down to the wire. Did Alex remember to ask you to bring your address book, Mary Beth?
MARY BETH. Yes. It's in the shopping bag. I brought a scrapbook I kept in high school, too. I thought you might get a kick out of looking at it.

(JULIA goes to the credenza and takes a scrapbook and address book

from the shopping bag.)

SUZANNE. Oh, Lord, if we're going to stroll down memory lane, I'd better sit down.

(She takes her coffee and sits on the SL chair at the table. TIM takes the chair SR of the table and sits on it behind MARY BETH's chair where he can continue to look over her shoulder.)

TIM. I noticed Pauline Grant isn't on the list. Wonder whatever happened to her.
SUZANNE. I think she died.
MARY BETH. No, she didn't — she moved to Scranton, Pennsylvania.
SUZANNE. Same thing.
MARY BETH. We exchange Christmas cards. I got one from her last week. She wrote she'll be in town to visit her folks. Her address is in my book, Julia.
JULIA. Great. I'll copy it down. That's one more off our "missing in action" list.

(JULIA will take a pad and pencil from the desk and carry them, the address book, and scrapbook to the table. She'll get her coffee and sit on the US chair there. She will copy an address from the book onto the pad. SUZANNE will leaf through the scrapbook.)

TIM. Oh, God — Wilton Hackett.
ALL. *(Making a motion suggesting poking a finger down their throats and gagging.)* Hack ... hack ... hack ... hack ...
SUZANNE. Tell me Hack's not going to be here.
MARY BETH, TIM & JULIA. *(Together.)* He's going to be here.
SUZANNE. Gag a maggot.
JULIA. Our class weirdo was the first to confirm. Then, when I came up after work yesterday, I had another message from him: "I haven't forgotten you after all these years. I'm on my way. Hack."
MARY BETH. He's on his way? Two weeks early? What's he doing — hitchhiking?

THE REUNION 21

SUZANNE. Sounds like he has a "thing" for you, Julia. I mean, if he "hasn't forgotten you after all these years ... "

JULIA. Oh, please ...

TIM. Why would he want to come back? Nobody in the entire school could stand him. Everyone treated him like shit. You'd think Hack would never want to see any of us again.

SUZANNE. Yeah — even I turned him down for a date.

TIM. Suzanne, my admiration for you just went up twelve points.

SUZANNE. For a grand total of ...?

TIM. Thirteen.

SUZANNE. *(Shooting him a bird.)* Fink.

(She goes back to scanning the scrapbook.)

MARY BETH. According to this, he's coming alone.

SUZANNE. That's, no doubt, the story of his life.

(TIM chuckles.)

MARY BETH. I don't get it.

TIM. Neither does he.

(SUZANNE smiles.)

MARY BETH. Huh?

JULIA. They're talking about his sex life, Mary Beth.

MARY BETH. *(Giggling in spite of herself.)* Shame on you! Maybe Hack has changed since high school.

JULIA. I doubt it. *(To TIM and MARY BETH.)* Look what he does for a living. *(To SUZANNE.)* He's a morgue attendant.

MARY BETH. Eee-uuuu....

SUZANNE. Gross! If I drop dead, squirt lighter fluid on me and cremate me on the spot! Whatever you do, DON'T send me to the morgue!

TIM. Fourteen points.

(SUZANNE shoots him another bird.)

THE REUNION

JULIA. Don't worry, he doesn't live in Cleveland anymore. He moved to San Francisco.

MARY BETH. *(Looking at the screen.)* Oh, yeah....How did you find his address, Julia?

SUZANNE. WHY did you find it?

JULIA. To tell the truth, I didn't go out of my way to get it, but when his cousin, Betsy Trotter, heard about the reunion, she called and gave me his e-mail address.

SUZANNE. I never could stand Betsy Trotter.

JULIA. She said her aunt, Mildred Hackett — Hack's mother — and Mr. Hackett died the summer after we graduated. Their house burned to the ground in the middle of the night with them inside it. They were charred to a crisp. Hack was the only one who got alive. He wasn't harmed.

MARY BETH. But his folks.... That's awful. How did the fire start?

JULIA. Betsy said no one is sure how it started. She told me Hack left town soon after that. He used the insurance money and his inheritance to move to San Francisco.

TIM. I didn't know he wasn't around anymore.

MARY BETH. Me, neither, but, to be honest, who of our classmates would have wanted to keep up with him?

SUZANNE. None. Couldn't you have conveniently lost ol' Hack's e-mail address, Julia?

JULIA. I considered it, but what if Betsy asked me about it at the reunion? Besides, that would be a tacky thing for the class valedictorian to do.

TIM. As I recall, if your grade point average had been a decimal point lower, Hack would have beat you out of the position.

MARY BETH. What a nightmare that would have been!

TIM. Well, we can't deny Hack was smart ... and a whiz at computers. A morgue attendant ... I'm surprised he didn't get a job as a computer programmer at a big corporation like IBM.

JULIA. He'd never make it past the interview. I mean, I wouldn't hire him, I don't care how smart he is. Would you?

TIM. Nope. You're right — he's too weird.

MARY BETH. I thought computer nerds were supposed to be

THE REUNION 23

weird — I thought it was a requirement.
SUZANNE. Mary Beth, there's a hierarchy of losers. It goes from "strange" to "oddball," then "nerd" and "weirdo." Hack goes off the top of the chart. If I had to label him, the word that comes to mind is "scary." I'd say he ended up working in a morgue by default; there he's surrounded by the only people who could stand to be around him — dead ones.
MARY BETH. *(She shivers.)* A goose just walked over my grave.
TIM. It doesn't bother me to be around the deceased, but the morgue is one section of the hospital I avoid if I can help it. I'll warn you — not only will Hack still look and act creepy, no doubt, now he won't smell so good either.
MARY BETH. What do you mean?
TIM. Formaldehyde ... if you're around it very long, the stench gets into your pores. Some of the cadavers they bring in are none too fresh, either, and that smell ...
JULIA. *(Cutting in.)* We get the idea.
MARY BETH. Double eee-uuu ...
SUZANNE. Gee, this conversation makes for a fun evening! Somebody change the subject.
JULIA. How about a good laugh?
SUZANNE. I'd KILL for a good laugh!
MARY BETH. That sounds peculiar ... but I could stand a little humor, too.
JULIA. *(Rising.)* All right ... but remember, you asked for it.

(She crosses to DL and checks the slide projector on the cart.)

TIM. A slide projector? Uh-oh.... What have you been up to?
JULIA. *(Crossing to UL.)* Move over to the table where you can see.

(TIM will return his chair to SR of the table and sit. MARY BETH will cross to the DS chair and sit. Both bring their coffee. SUZANNE adjusts her chair to watch. JULIA crosses to UL, closes the bathroom door, then snaps the light switch by the other doorway. The main lights go out, leaving the glow from the florescent tube over

the sink, the floor lamp and the light from the computer screen. Then JULIA will return to the projector.)

SUZANNE. I don't suppose there's any chance you've put together a porno slide show?
TIM. Suzanne, you have a one-track mind.
SUZANNE. I can't help it — I haven't had sex in forty-eight hours.
MARY BETH. Lucky you! I ... *(Stopping abruptly.)* Never mind.
JULIA. I thought it might be fun to put a screen in the gym and have these flashing on it when people arrive. I can set the slide carousel to run continuously on its own.

(She kneels on the floor and turns on the projector. A slide of ALEX projects onto the bathroom door. The slides should be of the cast ten years ago. Ideally, you should made the slides from the actors' actual high school graduation photos. A couple of slides of other students are needed as well.)

MARY BETH. It's Alex! That's his graduation photo!
SUZANNE. You didn't ...
JULIA. I did. I had my graphics department make slides of the entire class, from our yearbook.
SUZANNE. That's sadistic, you know that?
JULIA. If I save them to show at our twenty year reunion, THAT will be sadistic. This year it will just be amusing.
SUZANNE. Hardy-har-har...
TIM. I think it's a neat idea.

(JULIA advances to a slide of TIM.)

JULIA. We go from student body president to vice-president ...
TIM. Hey, what a good-looking guy!
SUZANNE. Let's all memorize Tim's hair. In a few years, it might be nothing BUT a memory.
TIM. That hurts!
MARY BETH. Don't be mean, Suzanne.
TIM. That's okay. I might go bald, but I'll never need to worry

THE REUNION

about having boobs hanging down to my patellas — that's "kneecaps" to you civilians.

MARY BETH, SUZANNE & JULIA. *(Together.)* Tim!

SUZANNE. Another remark like that and I'll kick your balls up to your nostrils.

TIM. Ouch!

JULIA. Moving right along ... *(She changes to a slide of MARY BETH.)* Our student body secretary, Mary Beth Clark.

MARY BETH. Speaking of hair, did mine really look like that?

SUZANNE. Yes, dear, but none of us had the heart to tell you.

(JULIA changes to a slide of SUZANNE.)

JULIA. Our treasurer ...

TIM. Hey, I think I've seen that picture recently - on a wanted poster in the post office. I guess somebody finally figured out what you did with the class funds, huh, Suzanne?

SUZANNE. What do you do, Tim? Practice your stand-up comic routine while you're slicing into patients' chests?

TIM. Sure, and if I goof, well, they can die laughing.

(The others groan.)

JULIA. And here's *moi*.

(She changes to a slide of herself.)

TIM. Beautiful...

MARY BETH. Gorgeous...

SUZANNE. Oh, well, no wonder you don't mind having YOUR picture splashed up on the wall.

JULIA. Cool it, you guys. I put ours first — I'll arrange the other photos in alphabetical order later.

(She changes to a slide of a girl.)

MARY BETH. Bonnie Zachery ... I think I heard she has three kids now.

THE REUNION

JULIA. One for each husband.
MARY BETH. No! Really?
JULIA. You'd be surprised what I've learned about our classmates while getting this thing together.
SUZANNE. Which you are honor-bound to share with the committee. I'd love to hear some dirt about somebody other than me.
TIM. Whatever Julia tells us, you hold the record, Suzanne, and always will.
SUZANNE. I'd shoot you another bird, Tim, but I'm giving my finger a rest.

(JULIA changes to a slide of a boy.)

MARY BETH. Who's that?
TIM. Robbie ... something ...
JULIA. Robbie Langford. Truck driver. Divorced. Not coming.

(She changes to a slide of WILTON HACKETT. He looks like a disturbed young man. He wears thick-lens glasses and has acne. His hair is a shambles. He has a feral look about the eyes. This one slide will have to be made of the actor who plays Wilton, made up in character with a wig. All stare at the slide a beat, then:)

TIM. *(Softly.)* Hack...
SUZANNE. The aforementioned Wilton Hackett.... My God, was he a loser...
MARY BETH. I had forgotten how ... disturbing ... his eyes looked ...

(There is the SOUND of the ELEVATOR MOTOR activating. They jump, startled. The ELEVATOR will lower to the first floor, pause, then ascend to the fourth. The indicator arrow will reflect this.)

JULIA. Alex has arrived.
MARY BETH. He shouldn't be here for another hour or so.
JULIA. He's the only other one with a card key. It has to be him.

THE REUNION

MARY BETH. Julia, could we finish the slide show later?
SUZANNE. Like, MUCH later?
JULIA. All right.

(She turns off the projector, rises, and will cross to UL and turn on the room lights.)

TIM. Where was Alex?
MARY BETH. At a meeting with some other coaches. *(Rising.)* I hope nothing's wrong.

(She crosses to UR.)

JULIA. More coffee, anyone?
SUZANNE. Why not? *(She gives her cup to JULIA.)* Black.
TIM. *(Rising and getting his cup.)* I'll fix mine.

(He and JULIA go behind the bar. JULIA fills Suzanne's cup and returns it to her. TIM fills his and doctors it at the bar. There is a DING and the elevator doors open. ALEX DAWSON is there. Alex is a large, stockily-built man, a high school P.E. teacher and football coach. He lives for sports. He wears a track suit and a warm-up jacket, maybe with a logo patch on it — cougar, tiger, whatever. He steps out of the elevator, ENTERING. The doors close behind him. He looks upset.)

MARY BETH. It is you, Alex.... What's wrong? What happened at the meeting?
ALEX. We called it off. Charley Dixon wasn't there.

(He takes off his jacket and tosses it onto the credenza.)

TIM. *(At the bar.)* Charley Dixon who was two years ahead of us? Great half-back?
MARY BETH. Millie's big brother?
ALEX. Yeah. Hi, Tim ... Julia ... Suzanne ... *(They ad-lib "hi's.")* Charley teaches at Northeast High School, coaches their foot-

ball team. Anyway, he had a neighbor call the school board office where we were meeting, tell us Charley and his wife had to go to Chicago. Emergency...

JULIA. Chicago? That's where Millie lives now. She e-mailed me a couple of weeks ago she and her husband, Phillip something ... Phillip Wilson ... are coming in for the reunion. I remember she has a cute call sign: philsmill.

ALEX. I'm afraid they're not going to make it.

MARY BETH. Why...?

ALEX. Millie's dead. *(The others react, shocked.)* So is her husband.

TIM. Oh, God.... A car accident?

ALEX. They were murdered. *(The others ad-lib reactions.)* Somebody stabbed them to death. They were struck repeatedly. Whoever told Charley said they were literally slaughtered.

SUZANNE. Dear God, somebody told him that over the phone!?!

ALEX. Apparently, they were killed last night, but the bodies weren't discovered until a couple of hours ago. *(MARY BETH groans and sways. ALEX takes her arm and seats her on the desk chair.)* I'm sorry, honey.

JULIA. Who could do such a thing...?

TIM. Probably a maniac. Do you know if they were robbed, or anything?

ALEX. They don't think so. The police said there were no signs of forced entry.

JULIA. If no one broke in, it must have been someone they knew.

TIM. Sounds logical...but then, it could have been someone posing as a pizza man, or ... I don't know ...

JULIA. I'll send flowers to the funeral and sign it for the class.

TIM. I'll chip in.

SUZANNE. Ditto.

ALEX. Us too. The coaches at the meeting took up a collection to get something for Charley. His baby sister ... damn shame ...

SUZANNE. Shit! Life sucks sometimes. She wasn't even thirty.

MARY BETH. Were there...? Did they have children?

JULIA. No. No children. She wrote me about their pair of Siamese cats.

THE REUNION 29

MARY BETH. I'm glad there were no kids. I mean ...
ALEX. We know what you mean, honey.

(MARY BETH starts to cry.)

MARY BETH. I liked Millie ...

(JULIA takes a napkin from the bar and crosses to MARY BETH.)

TIM. Yeah. Sweet girl ...
JULIA. *(Handing MARY BETH the napkin.)* Use this. It's all right.

(MARY BETH wipes her eyes and nose.)

ALEX. Sorry to bring bad news.
JULIA. *(Squeezing his arm.)* Have some coffee.
MARY BETH. Go ahead — I'm okay.

(He puts his hands on her shoulders from behind and kisses the top of her head. Then he follows JULIA behind the bar. She pours him coffee.)

ALEX. So, what have you guys been talking about?
SUZANNE. Hair.
ALEX. Hair? The musical?
JULIA. No, the follicle. The women's styles, and the men's abundance, or lack thereof.

(MARY BETH dries her eyes and swivels to face SL.)

TIM. Suzanne predicts I'll probably be bald by the twenty year reunion. She's a witch, so she probably knows what she's talking about.
SUZANNE. You better believe it. *(Waving her hands around toward TIM.)* Double, double, toil and trouble — turn Tim's hair into a stubble.

TIM. Thanks a lot, Suzanne. I guess I'd better call up tomorrow and make an appointment with Hair Club for Men. Could we get down to business, gang, before the woman turns me into a toad?

SUZANNE. I'll do that next time — I forgot my eye of newt.

(JULIA picks up the butcher knife and bangs the end of the handle on the bar like a gavel.)

JULIA. The meeting of the reunion committee is now in session!

(ALEX takes his cup, crosses, and sits on the chair DS of the table.)

ALEX. *(To MARY BETH.)* Honey, you want to join us?

MARY BETH. I'm fine here, Alex. This chair is great for my back.

JULIA. *(As she crosses to the chair US of the table and sits.)* Committee reports: Suzanne — entertainment ...

TIM. Yea! Great idea!

SUZANNE. I haven't given my report yet.

TIM. Oh, I thought Julia meant you were going to BE the entertainment.

SUZANNE. You wish ... and if you say, "Been there — done that," I swear I'll slap you! *(TIM holds up his hands, palms out, meaning "pass.")* Okay ... I've booked the deejay, C. D. Spinner.

MARY BETH. You're kidding.

SUZANNE. It's his professional name, Mary Beth. He's going to round up the top hits of ten years ago. He's very good, and he comes cheap. *(TIM looks as if he's about to say something. To him.)* Say it and you're dead meat!

JULIA. *(To MARY BETH.)* Is a deejay okay with you?

MARY BETH. Oh, sure. You know me — I'm easy. I'll go along with whatever the rest of you want to do.

JULIA. I'll report next. I've got the graphics department designing the memory book souvenir handouts, and my photographer has agreed to come to the dinner dance and shoot a group picture of the class. He'll take other photos on request for a reasonable fee.

ALEX. Good. My news is that the ball team and cheerleaders

THE REUNION 31

have volunteered to decorate the gym for us. *(The others clap.)* My students know that in no way will this affect their grades.

TIM. Yeah — right!

JULIA. Tim, how are donations coming in for the door prizes?

TIM. Not bad. Godwin's Jewelers donated a crystal bud vase for the person who travels the farthest to be here — small, but nice.

ALEX. How did you swing that?

TIM. Mr. Godwin is Eleanor's uncle.

SUZANNE. My uncle Morty is a butcher. I can try and hit him up for some pigs' feet.

TIM. If I get desperate enough, I'll get back to you. In addition to the vase, we've got a travel clock, a nice picture frame, and a hundred dollar savings bond for the graduate with the youngest baby … you know, for the kid.

JULIA. First babies often come early; you want to shoot for it, Mary Beth?

MARY BETH. It's a tempting thought.

ALEX. *(To MARY BETH's stomach.)* What do you say, Little Alex? If you give mommy a break and come out early, you'll get a hundred dollar savings bond.

MARY BETH. He said, "I don't think so, Dad."

SUZANNE. No new tax deduction for you guys this year.

JULIA. Oh, speaking of money, I received some more checks in the mail. *(Rising.)* I need to give them to you to deposit in our account, Suzanne. They're in that envelope by the computer, Mary Beth.

(She takes a step SR, but pauses when MARY BETH turns toward the computer and gasps.)

MARY BETH. If this is your idea of a joke, you have a warped sense of humor, Julia.

JULIA. What?

MARY BETH. Using that spooky graduation photo of Hack with "See you soon" written across the bottom as a screen saver.

(JULIA crosses with trepidation to behind MARY BETH and stares at the screen.)

32   **THE REUNION**

    ALEX. That sicko?
    SUZANNE. Yuck!
    TIM. Why would you put Hack's picture on your computer, Julia?
    JULIA. *(Softly.)* I didn't ...

(The others stare at JULIA, troubled, as she stares at the screen. The lights fade to:)

BLACKOUT

(Ominous music fades in and plays during the scene change. ALL exit.
STAGEHANDS strike the guests' coats and purses, leaving JULIA's coat on the coat rack; CALLIE's coat is added beside hers, and her purse with a handkerchief inside is placed on the desk. JULIA's purse with a lipstick and compact inside is placed on the bar. The shopping bag, yearbook and address book are struck, as well as the cups, saucers, spoons, cake, and napkins, including MARY BETH's. The pad and pencil are moved back to the desk; the knife is replaced in the block on the counter; the creamer and sugar bowl are replaced in the SR cabinet. The coffee pot is emptied and replaced on the coffee maker. The cart with the projector is moved against the wall SL, US of the tv. The switches to the florescent tube under the sink and to the lamp are turned off. The hand towels by the bathroom sink are struck. CALLIE enters in the dark and sits at the desk.)

Scene 2

(December 19. Friday. 6:40 p.m.
The music fades out as the lights fade up, including the glow from the computer. CALLIE, Julia's employee, is sitting at the computer which is on. CALLIE is in her 20's. Though neatly dressed in of-

THE REUNION 33

fice clothes, she probably spends more time at her computer than her mirror. She moves and clicks the mouse confidently. She stares a beat at the information she's brought up.)

CALLIE. *(Muttering to herself under her breath.)* Uh-huh ... just as I suspected.... You've been a very bad boy. *(Out loud, calling to off SL.)* There's no doubt about it, Ms. Jamison — you've been hacked.

JULIA. *(Entering SL. She is wearing slacks and a sweater or different blouse, and is putting on new earrings.)* I thought so. That's the only logical explanation for Hack's picture appearing on my computer.

CALLIE. Hack?

JULIA. That's what everyone called Wilton Hackett — the pin-up boy whose picture was on the screen. There's no telling how long it's been since he sent it. I've just gone in and out of the computer quickly for the last week or so, and haven't left it up long enough for the screen saver to appear. That fink!

CALLIE. Yes.... Definitely a fink.

JULIA. How did he do it? I thought you had to be on line before a hacker could get in and ... do their thing ... and I've barely booted up lately.

CALLIE. My guess is, when he got your e-mail address from the reunion announcement, he put you on his buddy list and kept it on the screen. When he saw the little red arrow by your name that indicated you were on line, he hacked in and created a "back door" he could use to come into your system and mess around whenever he wanted to. Even if I found it and closed it, he could come in again and create another one unless you change your e-mail address, which, with some servers, practically requires an act of Congress.

JULIA. Well, that's just great! I'll deal with Hack later; I don't have time tonight.

CALLIE. That's a nice outfit. Are you expecting someone?

JULIA. Suzanne Brinkerhoff, a classmate, is coming by after she gets off work. I meant to give her some checks for our reunion account last night, but when Hack appeared out of nowhere, so to speak, we forgot all about it. Anyway, Suzanne and I are going out for a bite to eat. You're welcome to join us.

CALLIE. Oh, no, ma'am. Thank you for asking, but Sylvester will be wondering where I am.

JULIA. I really appreciate your staying late, Callie. You'll get an overtime bonus in your next check.

CALLIE. I'm glad I could help. I didn't have any special plans for tonight. I'll stop by Blockbuster on my way home and rent some movies. Sylvester and I will cuddle up together and have our own film festival this weekend.

JULIA. *(Crossing to the desk.)* Callie, I'm sure Sylvester is an adorable cat, but wouldn't you rather have a nice guy to cuddle up with?

CALLIE. *(Shy.)* Oh, Ms. Jamison ...

JULIA. You'll never meet anyone cooped up in your apartment with Sylvester. Come with us. I'll treat.

CALLIE. It's kind of you to ask, but I couldn't. Maybe some other time ...

JULIA. Fine. Hey, I'm a lousy one to give advice about men. I haven't found one I want to keep, either. Perhaps I should get a cat, too, and forget about the two-legged animals. So, were you able to get rid of Hack?

CALLIE. Yes, ma'am. He had deleted your screen saver file and put his picture in its place. I took it out and used your original disks to put the scenic pictures back in. *(She looks at the screen.)* See? There's the one of wild flowers and butterflies.

JULIA. That's definitely an improvement. Hack didn't do any permanent damage, did he?

(She will cross above the bar, take a lipstick and compact from her purse, and apply fresh lipstick.)

CALLIE. I don't think so. I ran our latest virus scan disks through the computer. He didn't corrupt any files, as far as I can tell, or affect the hard drive. Still, Ms. Jamison, shouldn't you report this to the police? Computer hacking is a crime.

JULIA. I thought about it. When I realized what he'd done, I felt ... violated ... the same as if he had come into my home physically. After I calmed down, I figured it's probably just Hack's twisted idea

THE REUNION

of a prank. Besides, I can't prove Hack is the one who sent me his picture, even though I know it was him ... can I?

CALLIE. No, ma'am. With the right equipment, an expert can trace a hacker to his home site while his computer is linked to yours, but once he's signed off, it's very difficult.

JULIA. So, there you are. I have no proof. I guess as long as he didn't do any harm ...

CALLIE. If I were you, I'd consider changing my e-mail address so he can't get in again.

JULIA. I will, after the reunion. I'm still getting responses from my classmates, so I'll need to keep it until then.

CALLIE. Okay, but I hope you don't have any financial records in the computer with bank account numbers. I didn't see any ...

JULIA. I don't — that kind of information is in my computer at my lake home. I use a different e-mail address there. Very few people have it.

CALLIE. Good. You can't be too careful nowadays. I heard about ...

(The ELEVATOR MOTOR starts. The ELEVATOR descends to the first floor, pauses, then ascends back to the fourth. The dial reflects this.)

CALLIE. Ms. Brinkerhoff?

JULIA. Yes. She has a card key.

CALLIE. Your friend, what does she do?

JULIA. Suzanne? Anything that comes into her head, but if you mean for a living, she owns her own dress shop — designer fashions, very exclusive. Suzanne was our student body treasurer. She always did have good business sense.

CALLIE. Like you. I really admire successful business-women who make it on their own, Ms. Jamison.

JULIA. Thank you, Callie. To be honest, I'm very proud of Jamison Advertising. I've worked hard to make it one of Cleveland's most successful agencies, and I'll do whatever it takes to keep it on top.

CALLIE. Our clients love working with you. They're always commenting how smart you are, as well as attractive — and such a lady.

THE REUNION

JULIA. Even though it's a dog-eat-dog world, Callie, a woman doesn't have to be a bitch to succeed.

CALLIE. Yes, ma'am. I'd like to think that someday I could ... well ... you know ...

JULIA. You'll do fine, Callie. You're intelligent, and your computer skills are first-rate. All you need is a little self-confidence.

CALLIE. I'm working on it ...

(JULIA replaces the lipstick and compact into her purse. There is a DING and the elevator doors open. SUZANNE enters. She wears a coat over a stylish business outfit and carries a purse. She crosses to DR where JULIA meets her.)

SUZANNE. Well, I'm here. I would have been up five minutes ago, but I kept trying to open the door downstairs with a charge card until I finally realized I was holding the wrong piece of plastic. *(To CALLIE.)* Hi. I'm Suzanne Brinkerhoff, Julia's idiot classmate ... and not even a savant, at that.

JULIA. Suzanne, this is Callie Morris.

CALLIE. *(Rising.)* Hello.

SUZANNE. Nice to meet you. *(They shake hands.)* So you're the computer nut Julia's told us so much about. Been getting any lately?

CALLIE. *(Embarrassed.)* Oh! I...uh ...

SUZANNE. Me, neither.

JULIA. I should have warned you, Callie — Suzanne could be the poster model for sexually liberated women.

SUZANNE. Hey, I figure use it or lose it.

JULIA. I take it your date last night didn't pan out?

SUZANNE. *(Crossing to the table and laying down her purse.)* Ramon was a real loser. He had a few drinks and passed out on me. I didn't really care. After Hack's surprise appearance, I wasn't in the mood anyway, so I rolled out from under Ramon, got dressed, and went home.

CALLIE. My goodness ...

SUZANNE. Hey, it happens. You've both had that experience too, right?

CALLIE. Uh ... no ... not really ...

SUZANNE. Lucky you.

JULIA. I'm not talking.

SUZANNE. Well, shit. I was hoping to hear all the sordid details about your sex life over dinner. I'll tell you mine if you tell me yours.

JULIA. Suzanne, I already know more about your sex life than I want to.

SUZANNE. Spoil sport. *(Noticing the computer screen; crossing past CALLIE and JULIA to above the desk.)* How ... pastoral. I take it you wiped out Hack, figuratively speaking ... unfortunately ...

CALLIE. Yes ...

JULIA. Callie discovered he hacked into my computer, as we figured. She put my original screen savers back on.

SUZANNE. My screen savers are pics of Chippendale's hunks, but whatever turns your crank. Wonder what Hack has on his computer? Copies of Hieronymus Bosch's paintings?

JULIA. I wouldn't doubt it.

CALLIE. Who?

SUZANNE. The artist. He did really weird shit — the kind of stuff Hack would probably create if you turned him loose with a set of Crayolas.

JULIA. Can we talk about something else? We're going to have to face Hack soon enough at the reunion. I'd really like to put him out of my mind till then.

SUZANNE. I'm with you. I'm famished. Ready to eat?

JULIA. Sure. Oh, wait, the checks ...

(She steps to the desk and picks up the envelope.)

SUZANNE. I'm glad you thought of them. My memory is getting as short as Ramon's.... *(Looking at CALLIE.)* Never mind. Someday soon I'm going to have to choose between booze and brain cells. I've already got to the point where I'd forget my head if it weren't attached to my body.

JULIA. A check came in today from Carl Ditmore. Let me mark him paid before I forget that.

(She gives SUZANNE the envelope, then uses the mouse to bring up

the file. SUZANNE puts the envelope into her purse and lays it back on the table.)

SUZANNE. Julia and I are going to try a new Indian restaurant that just opened on Coventry Road. The Fig Tree. Their curry dishes are guaranteed to paralyze your taste buds. Want to join us?

CALLIE. Ms. Jamison invited me, but I need to get home. Thank you, anyway.

JULIA. That's odd ...

SUZANNE. What?

JULIA. Millie Dixon's information is on the chart right below Carl Ditmore's. Where I indicate if they're coming to the reunion, it says "no." I'm sure I typed in "yes" when I first heard from Millie.

CALLIE. Millie Dixon? The classmate you told me just got murdered?

JULIA. Yes.

(CALLIE and SUZANNE step SR and look over her shoulder at the computer.)

SUZANNE. You must have made a mistake.

JULIA. But I marked her "paid" when I got her check. You'd think I would have noticed then.... *(She opens a desk drawer and takes out two stacks of paper, each held together with a paper clip; one is thick, one thin. She drops the thick stack onto the desk.)* I ran a hard copy of the file to use when we set the place cards at the banquet. *(She flips a page.)* There ... see? Phillip and Millie Dixon Wilson — are attending — paid December third.

SUZANNE. Hack.

JULIA. What?

SUZANNE. It had to have been Hack. While he was in your system, he must have screwed around with the reservation list.

JULIA. *(To CALLIE.)* Could he do that?

CALLIE. Yes.... He could have changed it, copied it, deleted it ...

JULIA. Damn!

SUZANNE. There's no telling what info Hack has switched around. Now we can't be sure who's coming or who's not — or if they've paid ... not the ones who have responded since you printed that list, anyway. Wait till I get my hands on the bastard — I'll kick his ass all the way back to San Francisco.

JULIA. I know who's paid ... *(She picks up the thin stack.)* I made a list of all the checks we've deposited, including the batch I just gave you, and have kept it updated as they came in.

SUZANNE. Thank God! I have a confession to make, Julia. In school, you made so many lists I came to the conclusion you were finicky to the point of being anal-retentive. Now I'm glad you're a tight-ass perfectionist.

JULIA. Thank you, Suzanne ... I think ...

SUZANNE. We can cross-reference your bank deposit list against the information in the computer and undo Hack's handy-work, the shithead. *(Starting to take off her coat.)* It looks like dinner will be delayed ...

CALLIE. No, wait ... I'll check it for you. You go on to the restaurant ...

SUZANNE. The Fig Tree ...

CALLIE. The Fig Tree.

JULIA. Callie, that's sweet of you, but ...

CALLIE. *(Cutting in.)* I'll be through in no time. I can make corrections if any are needed, then copy the file onto a floppy disk. You can add new information to the floppy as it comes in and work from it until the reunion. That way, this Hack-person can't corrupt the file again.

SUZANNE. Julia, this woman deserves a promotion.

JULIA. That sounds like a distinct possibility.

CALLIE. Oh, Ms. Jamison, you don't have to ...

JULIA. *(Cutting in.)* Callie, a little advice from one business woman to another: there are times when it's wise to shut up. Shut up.

(She hands CALLIE the papers.)

CALLIE. *(Pleased.)* Yes, ma'am.

(CALLIE sits back down at the desk. She'll take the paper clip off the list and get ready to work at the computer.)

JULIA. *(To SUZANNE.)* I'll get my coat. *(She crosses to the coat rack, takes her coat and puts it on.)* Suzanne, will you grab my purse? It's on the bar.

SUZANNE. Sure.

(She takes her purse from the table, then picks up Julia's purse from the bar, and crosses to JULIA. JULIA turns on the floor lamp SL of the elevator.)

JULIA. Callie, you can turn the overhead lights out when you go. Just leave the lamp on.

CALLIE. Yes, Ms. Jamison.

(JULIA pushes the elevator button. Its doors open. SUZANNE hands her her purse.)

JULIA. Give Sylvester a hug for me.

(She and SUZANNE enter the elevator.)

CALLIE. I will.

SUZANNE. Sylvester, huh? Callie, you little devil! This Sylvester — is he sexy?

(JULIA pushes a button off SL of the elevator interior.)

CALLIE. *(Without turning around to look at SUZANNE.)* He's been neutered.

(SUZANNE gives CALLIE a startled look as the elevator doors close. The MOTOR activates and the elevator descends to the first floor. The dial indicates this. CALLIE gets a thought, stops, picks up the phone and punches in a number. She holds for several rings at the other end, then:)

CALLIE. Sylvester? It's Mommy. Are you listening to the answering machine? Mommy is sorry she's late. She has a little more

THE REUNION 41

work to do, then she'll pick up some movies and come right home. You be a good kitty. Mommy loves you. *(She makes kissing sounds.)* See you soon, Sylvester. *(She hangs up. CALLIE mutters to herself as she works.)* Where to start? *(She picks up the thick stack of papers and looks through them.)* E-mail messages ... Ms. Jamison made hard copies of all her classmates' messages.... Confirming ... confirming ... regrets ... *(Stopping at one page.)* Millie Dixon Wilson... *(Reading.)* "Hi, Julia. It's great hearing from you. Yes, I'll attend! I'm dying to see you and all the others at the reunion, and to introduce you to my wonderful husband! I'll put our check in the mail tomorrow. Lots of affection, Millie." That poor woman ... "philsmil" ... They must have really loved each other. *(She takes a handkerchief from her purse on the desk and wipes her eyes, then flips through some more papers.)* I can use these to make sure the confirmations are correct on the file, then I'll refer to the bank deposit list to mark them paid or not. *(She stops at another page.)* Wilton Hackett. *(Reading.)* "Beautiful Julia ... Though I didn't realize it until I got your e-mail, seeing all my old classmates again is the answer to a dream. I'm sure this reunion will be one no one ever forgets. See you soon. Hack." What's your call sign? "Wilhack at SanFran." Oh yes, Ms. Brinkerhoff mentioned you live in San Francisco. *(She flips to the next page.)* Another one? *(Reading.)* "I haven't forgotten you after all these years. I'm on my way. Hack" ... sent ... the day before yesterday. I guess I can put you down as a definite confirmation. *(She turns to the computer, then stops as she realizes something. She looks back at the page, flips to the one before it, then back to the second.)* "philsmil" ... You sent the second message from Millie Dixon's computer ... the day she ... oh, no! ... oh, golly! ... oh, no! ... *(Frightened.)* You were there in her house! You were ... *(Rising.)* I've got to show these to Ms. Jamison! She'll need to notify ... oh, golly! *(She drops the sheets onto the desk, rushes to the coat rack, grabs her coat, and pushes the elevator button. The ELEVATOR MOTOR starts. The elevator will ascend from the first floor. The dial indicates this. CALLIE hurries into her coat.)* They were going to ... what did Ms. Brinkerhoff say...? The Fig Tree! She said it's on Coventry Road ... *(She rushes to the desk and grabs her purse.)* Oh! The e-mails... *(She grabs the two pages from Hack, then hurries back to the elevator, trying to stuff them into her purse.)* The lights ...

(She flips the light switch. The overhead lights go out, leaving illumination from the floor lamp and computer screen. There is a DING and the elevator doors open behind her. CALLIE steps sideways back into the elevator, facing SL, still stuffing the papers into her purse, and hits the unseen button off left. She turns forward. WILTON HACKETT steps from off right to behind her. He grabs the hair on the top of her head with one hand, pulling her head back, and slashes a knife across her throat with the other. She drops her purse. Blood appears at the wound as the doors slide shut. The lamp and computer screen fade to:)

BLACKOUT

(Ominous music fades in and plays a few beats. During the blackout, Callie's purse is struck from the elevator. A STAGEHAND takes the butcher knife from its block, wets it, and leaves it in the sink.)

Scene 3

(10:55 p.m.

The music fades out as the floor lamp and computer screen fade up. The ELEVATOR MOTOR starts. The elevator descends to the first floor, pauses, then ascends back to the fourth. The dial reflects this. There is a DING and the doors slide open. JULIA and SUZANNE ENTER, wearing their coats and carrying their purses.)

JULIA. *(Laughing.)* So, when you see Sarah at the reunion, are you going to tell her you're the one who stole the garter snake from the biology lab and put it in her locker?

(She flips the light switch; the overhead lights come on. She and SUZANNE will put their purses on the credenza, remove their coats and hang them on the rack. The elevator doors close behind them.)

THE REUNION 43

SUZANNE. No, and don't you tell her, either. I only did it because she used to elbow me in the ribs in P.E. when we played basketball and were on opposite teams. If she were to find out I'm the one who made her wet her pants in a crowded hallway between classes, she might come at me with those bony elbows again.

JULIA. Your secret is safe with me.

SUZANNE. Speaking of wetting one's pants ...

JULIA. The facilities are all yours.

SUZANNE. *(Crossing to the bathroom.)* You must think I have the kidneys of a two month old, but you know what? That aspirin I took at the restaurant? I think I swallowed one of my water pills by mistake.

JULIA. Go! Go!

(SUZANNE exits into the bathroom and closes the door. JULIA crosses behind the bar, takes a glass on the counter by the sink and starts to turn on the faucet. She stops, puts down the glass, and picks the wet butcher knife from the sink. She looks at it, puzzled, not expecting to find it there. She shakes the water off, takes a dish towel, dries the knife, and puts it back into the butcher block. She takes the glass, runs some water into it from the faucet, and takes a drink. There is the SOUND of a TOILET FLUSHING. SUZANNE opens the bathroom door. Remaining inside, she and JULIA talk without seeing each other.)

SUZANNE. Now I'm SURE I took a Lasix!

(She turns on the water at the sink and washes her hands.)

JULIA. Then I'm glad we made it back in time.

(She takes a sip of water.)

SUZANNE. I love your apartment, Julia, but it's a shame there was no way to put a window here in the bathroom to air it out. *(Looking off SL.)* There's still a lot of water standing in the tub.

(She turns off the water, takes a hand towel, and dries her hands.)

JULIA. Really? It usually evaporates in a couple of hours. How about some coffee? I can make a pot — decaffeinated, if you prefer?

(She reaches up behind her and grips the handle of the SL cabinet door above the sink, not looking at it. She opens the door. The can of coffee is gone; in its place is CALLIE'S severed head, blood around the neck where it was cut off; blood also runs from her nose and mouth. There is a wide-eyed, terrified expression frozen on her face. [SEE PRODUCTION NOTES FOR THIS SPECIAL EFFECT.])

SUZANNE. I'd better pass if I want to make it home without pulling the car over and squatting at the curb.

(She tosses the towel onto the sink and enters from the bathroom just as JULIA closes the cabinet door without ever looking at it. SUZANNE narrowly misses seeing the head.)

JULIA. That's probably a good idea. I'd hate to hear you got arrested for indecent exposure.
SUZANNE. Honey, it wouldn't be the first time. *(JULIA laughs.)* Hey, thanks for the dinner. Next time it'll be on me.
JULIA. *(Coming around the bar and meeting her DS of it.)* Fine, and I want there to be a next time. I had forgotten how much fun you are to be around. Let's not lose touch again, Suzanne.
SUZANNE. We won't, and that's a promise. Men come and go — no pun intended — but a good, reliable girlfriend is hard to find. Friends?
JULIA. Friends.

(They give each other a warm, friendly hug.)

SUZANNE. It's getting late. I'd better head home.

JULIA. If you must.

THE REUNION 45

(JULIA links SUZANNE's arm through hers, and walks her to the coat rack UR. SUZANNE will put on her coat.)

SUZANNE. I must. I want to get up early in the morning — by noon, at least — and hit the stores. I made a vow to get my Christmas shopping finished before the last minute this year.

JULIA. Mine's done. I ordered nearly all of my gifts on the computer. Callie showed me dozens of web sites for arm chair shoppers. A few clicks of the mouse and you can buy anything from baby rattles to battleships.

SUZANNE. Smart girl — Callie's obviously got a good head on her shoulders. Better hold on to her.

JULIA. I plan to.

SUZANNE. *(Picking up her purse.)* Well, I'm outta here.

JULIA. Be careful on your way home.

SUZANNE. Don't worry — I keep a gun in my glove compartment in the car.

JULIA. A gun? I'd probably shoot myself in the foot.

SUZANNE. You don't have one? For protection?

JULIA. Not me. Guns make me nervous.

SUZANNE. Then that's something you're going to have to overcome. We'll sign you up for a course at the firing range. It's great. I took it. In fact, the hunk that was teaching it and I ...

JULIA. *(Cutting in.)* Suzanne!

SUZANNE. Right. *(She pushes the button. The elevator doors open.)* We'll save that story till next time. Bye, sweetie. *(They hug. SUZANNE steps into the elevator and pushes the button off SL. The doors start to close.)* I'll call you next week.

(The doors close. The ELEVATOR MOTOR starts. The elevator descends to the first floor, then stops. The dial indicates this. JULIA turns out the floor lamp SL of the elevator, then crosses to the desk.)

JULIA. *(Muttering to herself.)* Nice screen saver, Callie, but you could have turned it off — I've had enough of computers for one day. *(She touches the space bar on the keyboard; she looks at the screen, surprised.)* Not another e-mail ... *(Reading.)* "I'm closer than you think. Hack." *(Sarcastically.)* Great. *(She makes some clicks with the mouse, then pushes the power button. The screen goes dark.)* Suzanne was right — I should have "lost" his e-mail address. *(She rubs her neck and rotates her head, loosening the muscles.)* Wilton Hackett, you really are a pain in the neck. Maybe I should check and see if you've been screwing around in my computer again. Coffee ... *(She crosses behind the bar. She removes the coffee pot from its base, fills it with water from the faucet, then sets it on the counter. She reaches up to the cabinet over the sink. When her fingers touch the door handle, the PHONE RINGS. She jumps, startled, then crosses back to the desk.)* It's a little late to be calling, isn't it? *(She picks up the receiver.)* Hello ... hi, Mary Beth, what ...? ... no, it's not on ... *(She crosses to the cart DL and picks up the tv remote.)* What channel? *(Using the remote, she turns on the tv and changes the channel.)* Suzanne and I went out to dinner, so...

(ANNOUNCERS' VOICES come from the television.)

FEMALE NEWS ANCHOR: KIMBERLY (VOICE). ...but, thankfully, the fire fighters apparently have the blaze under control. We'll get back to you, Sharon, for an update later in the newscast. Al?

JULIA. What...?

MALE NEWS ANCHOR: AL (VOICE). We've re-established contact with our field reporter, Kimberly Tate, at the site of the gristly murder that occurred today in the Shaker Heights area.

JULIA. Mary Beth, who ...?

KIMBERLY (VOICE). *(There are ambient outdoor noises in the background.)* I'm here, Al, outside the home of Darren and Miranda Everett where earlier today a brutal murder took place.

JULIA. *(Overlapping the television.)* Miranda...? Randi? Randi Rawlins?

KIMBERLY (VOICE). *(Continuing without a break.)* According to police detective Lt. John Lawton, Mr. Everett arrived home from work about 6:00 p.m. tonight to discover the body of Mrs. Everett who had been stabbed to death. *(With a moan, JULIA sinks onto the chair.)* The Everetts' eleven month old daughter, Bonnie, was in the

THE REUNION

playpen, unharmed. Lt. Lawton, do you have any suspects at this point?

LT. LAWTON (VOICE). None at the moment, Ms. Tate, but the police will do everything in our power to apprehend the perpetrator.

KIMBERLY (VOICE). Lieutenant, have you found the murder weapon?

LT. LAWTON (VOICE). Yes. Indications are, Mrs. Everett was struck repeatedly by a butcher knife from her own kitchen. The killer then apparently ran the knife through the dishwasher while he, we believe, took a shower. The washing machine had been used as well — to remove blood from his clothes, we assume.

JULIA. I know, Mary Beth — it's terrible ...

KIMBERLY (VOICE). Is there anything else you can tell us, Lt. Lawton?

LT. LAWTON (VOICE). Not at this time. Whoever did this is a very sick individual. He will be captured.

KIMBERLY (VOICE). We certainly hope so. Al?

(JULIA clicks the remote, turning off the television. She rises and puts the remote back onto the cart.)

JULIA. I know it's upsetting, Mary Beth, but try not to cry ... I heard, almost a year old ... yes, her first Christmas ... I agree — both classmates within a few days of each other.... *(She crosses to the desk.)* That came to my mind as well. It's horrible to think it could be him.... I don't know ... they might think we're crackpots. I mean, what would we say? That this weird kid we went to school with is coming back to town, might well be here by now, so ... yes, Chicago is on the way from San Francisco, but...yes, Callie discovered he hacked into my data base — she was here tonight, working on it — but we can't prove it was Hack, and ... all right, maybe we should. The worse that could happen is they would think we're a pair of hysterical, over-imaginative women. So what? You're right. I'll call them tomorrow ... okay, Mary Beth.... Mary Beth, where's Alex?... Oh, good. Give him a hug for me ... you guys be careful ... yes ... bye ...

(She hangs up. WILTON HACKETT ENTERS SL. As we get our first

good look at him, we see that his wild hair is now cut close to his scalp. The acne has cleared up, leaving pits and scars on his sickly pale face. His glasses are different, but still require thick lenses. He is dressed in black pants, shirt, boots and an ankle-length, Western-style black coat. There are rings or studs pierced through his ears and/or nose and/or eyebrow.)

HACK. Hello, Julia.

(JULIA freezes a beat at the sound of his voice, then turns slowly to face him. They stare at each other as the lights fade to:)

BLACKOUT

CURTAIN

ACT II

Scene 1

(Immediately following.
(The music fades out as the curtain opens. Only a second has passed since the end of Act I. JULIA is at the desk; HACK is at the SL doorway.)

JULIA. Hack ...

HACK. I told you I was closer than you think. *(Crossing slowly to above the table.)* My God, you're even more beautiful than I remembered.

JULIA. How did you get into my apartment?

HACK. I could have hacked into the computerized keypad on your door lock downstairs, and on the elevator, but that takes time, and I didn't want to risk it that some cop in a passing patrol car would mistake me for a pothead attempting to break in. My particular vice doesn't happen to be drugs. So I found a more expedient way to let myself in.

JULIA. How...?

HACK. I borrowed Tim's card key.

JULIA. *(Sinking onto the desk chair. Fearful.)* Tim ...

HACK. *(Gripping the back of the chair US of the table.)* Tim Grant, student body vice president and all-around popular guy? *(He raises the chair a couple of inches and slams it down hard.)* God, he's such a fucking phoney! I could always see right through him!

JULIA. What do you mean?

HACK. You don't know?

JULIA. You didn't...?

HACK. Kill him? Fillet him? Not yet, although last night I was very tempted to get reacquainted with Tim and that slut Suzanne and super-jock Alex and his little wifey with the baby-filled belly, Mary Beth. I stood in the shadows down the street and watched them let themselves in with their card keys. I had come to pay you a visit, Julia, but decided to wait when I saw you had company. Let me guess — you student body officers were having a little meeting to plan the reunion, right?

JULIA. Yes. How did you know where to find me?

HACK. *(Crossing to her.)* Because you bragged about it, Julia, in the bios you've been composing in your computer for the reunion booklets. "Julia Jamison owns her own advertising agency in downtown Cleveland." Doing a bit of self-promotion, are we? "She lives in an apartment on the top floor during the week, but prefers to spend her weekends and holidays at her home at Bay Village on Lake Erie." My, my, what a charming way to rub it in, Ms. Jamison! What a very unsubtle way to say "Look how successful I am!"

JULIA. I wasn't ...

HACK. *(Cutting in.)* Bullshit! You know, your bragging was practically an invitation to visit, Julia, so I took you up on it ... and here I am.... Now that I'm here, I plan to stay a while. Tell me, Julia, how come a woman with your looks and intelligence never got married?

JULIA. Honest answer? I don't think I'd make a very good wife. My career comes first and always will. I love my work.

HACK. So do I.

JULIA. *(Rising.)* Hack ...

HACK. Sit down!

(JULIA sinks back onto the chair. She eyes the phone, but resists the temptation to grab it.)

JULIA. You were telling me about Tim ...

THE REUNION

HACK. Oh, yes. Well, when I saw that you use card keys to get into the building, I realized I needed to obtain one before I could get you alone for a quiet little *tête-à-tête*. *(He crosses to SL of JULIA.)* Your extremely useful biographical information said that Tim is a doctor now, and works at Metro General. This morning I paid a visit to Metro. I didn't bring many clothes for our reunion, but I did throw in some scrubs and the lab coat I wore at the morgue in San Francisco, including the photo I. D. we have to clip on. *(He touches his chest, indicating where.)* You know how it is, Julia.... When you look like you BELONG, no one questions your right to be there! Hell, I could have walked into an operating room, picked up a scalpel, and slit a patient open from sternum to groin, and nobody would have stopped me because I looked like I BELONGED! *(Moving about at will.)* The thing is, I can make an incision as precise as Dr. Tim can. I've had a lot of practice over the last ten years — self-taught, of course. I started honing my skills on cadavers — the homeless, the reprobates ... nobody pays any attention to what happens to their corpses. It was an edifying way to pass the time — all those thousands of hours we were alone together, my silent companions and I. Eventually I felt I had learned all I could from working with the deceased; it was time to move on to live specimens. Finding them is so easy in San Francisco, Julia — there are hundreds of street people, as well as prostitutes of both sexes, just waiting for me to find them, to touch them, to ... use them. Hundreds who don't "belong" in the kind of world you live in, you and your "elite" friends. *(He laughs.)* It's funny — sometimes the very people I "got acquainted with" in a dark alley one night showed up at my morgue the next morning. It was all I could do not to laugh in the faces of the police officers who brought them in. Once we were alone, I could "pick up where I had left off," so to speak. A lot of my "new-found friends" never surfaced, of course, not the ones I met near the bay. Never "surfaced"? The bay? Where's your sense of humor, Julia? *(She just looks at him.)* Enough digressing. I just thought you'd appreciate knowing how I've spent the last ten years. As I told you in my first e-mail, your news about the reunion was like the answer to a dream. It's the prefect opportunity for me to show all of you stuck-up fuckers what I'VE accomplished since high school! Where was I ...? Oh, yes, Tim's card key.... Wearing my working clothes, I breezed into the doctors' scrub room, picked the Mickey Mouse lock on Tim's locker, and borrowed the card from Tim's wallet while he was, we assume, on one of the floors above, saving lives right and left. He won't miss it. There won't be any more reunion committee meetings in your swanky apartment, Julia, because once I've finished with all of you, there won't be any more committee.

JULIA. Millie Dixon ... Randi Rawlins ... You murdered them too, didn't you?

HACK. Yes.

JULIA. Why?

HACK. They were beauty queens, like you, Julia — don't you remember? Millie was Homecoming Queen, Randi got her crown at the Valentine Dance. I wasn't at either event, naturally. It seems none of the girls at our school would date me. Call me an anarchist, but I believe royalty must pay a price, sooner or later. "Off with their heads!" Millie happened to live on my way here, and Randi ... well, this afternoon I had a little time to kill ...

JULIA. Oh, God.... *(Beat.)* You can't get away with it, Hack. You'll get caught. I'm not the only one who has figured out what you're doing.

HACK. You mean Mary Beth? *(He wanders into the kitchen area, looks in the sink, sees the knife isn't there, then sees it is in the butcher block, during:)* I heard you on the phone with her. I plan to drop in on the mother-to-be and Alex later tonight, after our visit — then Suzanne and Tim. I'll have to work quickly to make the rounds of the reunion committee. That's a shame — I would prefer to take my time and savor each encounter.... But don't worry, Julia — I won't rush things with you. You're the one I've looked forward to being with the most, my prom queen. That's why I let Suzanne leave a few minutes ago. I don't want anything to distract me, to take away from

THE REUNION

our reunion, yours and mine. *(The PHONE RINGS. JULIA jumps, startled. HACK freezes a beat.)* Don't answer it. *(JULIA is torn; she grabs the phone. HACK whips the butcher knife from the block.)* If you pick it up, I'll sever your hand from your wrist! *(JULIA removes her hand. They wait as the phone rings three or four more times, then stops.)* Another late call? Apparently, you're as popular as ever ... but you're going to be much too busy to chat on the phone.

JULIA. They'll know it's you! Someone will know!

HACK. *(Laying the knife on the chopping block SL of the sink and crossing to below the bar.)* I doubt it. Who else but the committee has given me a thought in years? Well, maybe Betsy — Cousin Betsy let me know she gave you my e-mail address. I suppose I should swing by and see sweet, stupid Betsy before I leave town. There are a few others I would love to work in, including a couple of teachers who made my life hell, as well. Even though I was the SECOND smartest student in our class — thanks to you — most of the faculty, the so-called adults who are supposed to judge us by our ABILITIES, not our appearance, treated me like a leper. Acne is no fun, Julia, but it's hardly a deadly, infectious disease.

JULIA. *(Rising.)* It wasn't just your appearance that turned people off, Hack — it was you! You — the person! You've always been sick ... *(Tapping her head.)* ... in here! You need help!

HACK. Thank you very much for that revealing analysis, Ms. Freud. The question is, was I always the way I am, or did you — all of you — make me this way? Which came first, the chicken or the egg? Does it really matter?

JULIA. Hack, let me call someone ... Tim! Tim must know some other doctors who can help you!

HACK. You mean shrinks? *(He laughs.)* They're a waste of time. My folks sent me to one. Didn't know that, did you? If you had, your crowd would have giggled behind my back about that too, wouldn't you? You know what I learned from that experience, Julia? I learned that shrinks are the most pompous, self-important assholes on this earth ... little tin gods! They like to pick at your brain ... pick, pick,

THE REUNION

pick! I'd rather die than be subjected to that kind of torture again! Any parent who puts their kid through that ... well ... *(JULIA stares at him a beat, then breaks and runs to the elevator. HACK runs after her. She hits the button; the doors slide open. HACK grabs her arm and flings her away from the elevator.)* You're not going anywhere, Julia! You never had time for me before, but, by GOD!, you're going to pay attention to me NOW! In case you get another urge to make an abrupt departure, let's send the elevator down to the ground floor — remove the temptation.

(He steps back into the elevator, pushes the button off SL, then steps back out. The doors slide shut behind him. The ELEVATOR MOTOR starts. The elevator descends to the first floor. The dial indicates this.)

JULIA. *(Holding her arm where he grabbed her and crossing slowly to above the table.)* Hack, what you say is true — we did treat you badly in high school. We were young and ... and ... foolish and inconsiderate. Our behavior was inexcusable, and I'm sorry. I don't know why we behaved like we did.

HACK. *(Crossing to DR.)* Oh, I know why, Julia — you were obeying the laws of nature. Among the lower orders of the animal kingdom, if a pup or cub in the litter is born weak or deformed or "not normal," the pack kills it, sometimes its own mother herself. "Survival of the fittest." You were simply following your instincts. Despite thousands of years of evolution, we're still a savage species. Our killer instinct is still there, just below the surface. "Go, team!" "Slay the wildcats!" "I made a killing in the stock market." "I'm going into that meeting and knock 'em dead!" I chose to let those feelings rise to the surface. The only difference between you and me, Julia, is that you wound with words and looks and laughs — I fight back with the modern world's equivalent of claws — the knife. There's no need to apologize for what you are. I don't.

JULIA. But human beings do have feelings that the other animals don't, feelings like compassion and forgiveness ...

HACK. If you say so. Personally, I haven't evolved that far up the ladder. I didn't know how to strike back when I was a scrawny, homely teenager, but I do now.

(He crosses to the coat rack UR, removing his coat.)

JULIA. Before you killed Millie and Randi, did you explain to them why you were doing it?

HACK. *(He hangs his coat on the rack, then crosses back DR, unbuttoning and rolling up his shirt sleeves.)* No. Why bother? They wouldn't have understood. You're the only one I've confided in, Julia. You're the only one as smart as I am ... the only one who might understand. Believe it or not, it's important to me that you do. You should feel honored.

JULIA. My understanding.... It won't change anything, will it?

HACK. No. You have to pay your debt, just like the others.

JULIA. Yet you think you won't? You think you can get away with multiple murders and not get caught?

HACK. I have for years.

JULIA. Those people in San Francisco — you said they were strangers. There was nothing to link them to you, and no one misses misfits, right? But killing your fellow classmates is different, and if you kill Betsy.... Betsy is your own cousin. The police will figure it out, Hack.

HACK. They might suspect me, but suspecting and proving are two different things. By the time the police put all the pieces together ... *(He chuckles.)* ... "Put all the pieces together?" ... by that time, I'll be back in San Francisco, cavorting with my cadavers, and nobody will be able to prove I was here. I told my very inferior superiors at work I was going to Tijuana for a few days. I go there often, for the bullfights. I love the bullfights. Once I saw a bull rip the matador's stomach open with its horns. The man's guts spilled out right out into the ring.

JULIA. If you try to murder us all, you'll never get away with it! You'll make a mistake! Just one slip is all it takes!

HACK. I did make one little error, but I can correct it. I'll be very careful not to let that happen again.

JULIA. An error? What error?

HACK. One that girl who was here noticed. An employee of yours?

JULIA. Callie?

HACK. Was that her name? *(JULIA flinches at his use of the past tense.)* I watched you and Suzanne leave earlier, then let myself in with Tim's key to wait for you to return. I had just slipped into the elevator when someone — Callie? — engaged it to come up to this floor. I bet she was on her way to show you her discovery.

JULIA. What discovery?

HACK. She had a copy of the first note I sent you which included my e-mail address, and also a copy of the message I sent from Millie's, after I finished with her and her husband. Millie was sending someone an e-mail when I arrived, and the file was still on the screen. I couldn't resist dashing off a few words to you before I left. It went out with Millie's e-mail address on it, of course. It was stupid of me not to realize it would, but I was so pumped up, so energized ... There's nothing like the smell of blood to make the adrenaline flow, Julia.... I won't make any more mistakes, though. Before I go, I'll wipe your hard drive clean, and set a fire to destroy any other paper copies of our correspondence you might have made. Yes, I think a fire is necessary.... Your body and the girl's must go up in flames.

JULIA. Callie.... Where is she?

HACK. Now, let me think.... *(He moves about SR as if searching for her.)* Callie? Where are you? Come out, come out, where ever you are! Where did I put you? Was it in the credenza? Or the kitchen cabinets? Or both? Want to help me find her, Julia?

JULIA. *(Queasy.)* No.

(She sinks onto the chair US of the table.)

THE REUNION 57

HACK. *(Crossing above her slowly to SL.)* You have to admit I do very neat work — no sign of a mess anywhere, is there? I cleaned the elevator where we 'met," then I finished getting to know her in the tub. All the sticky stuff went right down the drain. Afterward, I took a shower, of course. I stripped before getting down to business. I like to work naked. I like the way it feels to have warm blood all over my body, to have it drip off my genitals. It's very erotic.

JULIA. I'm going to be sick ...

(She rises and rushes to the sink. HACK moves quickly to her. JULIA sounds as if she is vomiting. He turns on the faucet and water rushes out. He splashes the water around the sink with his right hand.)

HACK. Poor baby.... Don't worry — a little water will wash it all away. *(JULIA grabs HACK's right wrist with her right hand and snaps on the switch SR of the sink with her left. The GARBAGE DISPOSAL UNIT ROARS to life. She then grabs his wrist with her left hand as well and uses both to shove HACK's hand into the drain. He screams as blood splatters both of them. He gives JULIA a backhanded slap with his left hand knocking her away a couple of steps. He hits the switch with his left hand and the GARBAGE DISPOSAL STOPS. He raises his right hand with it clinched into a bloody fist. [SEE PRODUCTION NOTES FOR THE SPECIAL EFFECT.])* YOU BITCH!!! YOU FUCKING BITCH!!!

(He grabs the dish towel by the sink and wraps it around his injured hand.)

JULIA. What's the matter, Hack!?! You love pain! You love blood! It's not the same when it's your own, is it!?!

HACK. *(Grabbing the knife from the counter with his left hand.)* You tell me, bitch!

(He slashes the knife toward her. JULIA backs away DS from him.

THE REUNION

The ELEVATOR MOTOR STARTS and the elevator rises to the fourth floor. The dial indicates this.)

JULIA. Help me! Somebody help me!

(She runs to the door SL with HACK right behind her. She grabs the knob, but realizes he's too near and turns to face him as he raises the knife to strike. She grabs his wrist. His strength is greater and he manages to inch the knife toward her face.)

HACK. I'm going to cut your beautiful face ... OFF!!!

(Suddenly, JULIA releases his wrist and steps DS; the knife swings down, missing her. She stumbles below the recliner and to below the table.)

JULIA. Help me!

(HACK crosses down between the table and recliner to her left, raising the knife.)

HACK. Die, bitch!

(JULIA screams. There is a DING and the elevator doors slide open. SUZANNE is there. She is wearing her coat. Her purse is in one hand, a gun in the other. She ENTERS, stepping out of the elevator, and fires the gun into the air over HACK's head. He freezes.)

SUZANNE. Don't move, asshole, or I'll blow your ugly head off!
JULIA. *(Stumbling to the desk, DR.)* Suzanne ... Thank God...
SUZANNE. I know how to use this, Hack. Put it down! Put the knife down now!
HACK. Anything you say, Suzanne. *(He slowly lowers the knife and drops it onto the table.)* We meet early. I wasn't planning our re-

union until later tonight.

SUZANNE. Sorry to disappoint you, you sick fuck. *(She lays her purse on the credenza. Noticing the blood on JULIA.)* Julia ...

JULIA. I'm okay. It's Hack's blood. I jammed his hand into the garbage disposal.

SUZANNE. Good for you!

(She notices the water running, crosses to sink, and turns off the faucet, keeping the gun on HACK the whole time.)

HACK. Actually, my hand hurts like hell. I would trouble you for some aspirin, but they're anticoagulants, so I suppose I'd better not.

JULIA. How did you know Hack was here?

SUZANNE. I guessed he might be. *(She crosses down to between HACK and JULIA.)* I was listening to the car radio on the way home and heard a news announcement about Randi Rawlins. She ...

JULIA. *(Cutting in.)* I know. I saw it on tv.

SUZANNE. Two of our classmates murdered when Hack comes home? His hacking into your computer? Too coincidental. Then it struck me — when we came back here after dinner, Callie had apparently left, but we had to call the elevator down from the apartment. If she had gone, why wasn't it on the first floor?

HACK. Because I'm stupid! *(He smacks his head with his hand.)* Stupid! Stupid! Stupid!

SUZANNE. Good of you to admit it. I called you from my cell phone, Julia, and when you didn't answer, I knew something was wrong. I got back here as fast as I could.

JULIA. Luckily for me. You saved my life.

SUZANNE. Callie?

JULIA. Hack said he killed her.

SUZANNE. You freak! *(To JULIA.)* It's not too late for me to shoot him and claim it was in self-defense.

HACK. Slicing up the girl was fun, but it wasn't personal ... like it would be with you, Suzanne. I hate to be rude and sit while there is a lady standing, to give you the benefit of the doubt, but now that that exquisite adrenaline rush Julia provided has passed, the old knees are feeling a little wobbly.

(He sits on the chair DS of the table.)

SUZANNE. He's still bleeding. Slowly bleeding to death is too good for you, scumbag. I'll call the police.

(She takes a step toward the desk.)

JULIA. No, wait ...

(SUZANNE stops. JULIA sits at the desk. She picks up the thick stack of papers, hesitates, pondering a decision, turns her head to stare at HACK a beat, then looks down at the pages.)

SUZANNE. What are you doing?
JULIA. I need the number ... *(She flips a couple of pages, then picks up the phone and dials a number she sees on the sheet. It rings on the other end a couple of times.)* Tim ... it's Julia ... sorry to wake you. I need you to come over right away. It's an emergency. Do you doctors still carry instruments in black bags?... Good. Bring it ... no, I'm all right. Tim, you'll need to ring the buzzer — your card key is gone. I'll explain when you get here ... thanks, Tim. Just hurry.

(She pushes the off button on the phone.)

SUZANNE. You called Tim?
JULIA. Hack came all this way for a reunion. We can't disappoint him, can we?

(SUZANNE and HACK stare at her as she flips to another page, stops, and starts to punch another number into the phone. The

THE REUNION 61

lights fade to:)

BLACKOUT

(Ominous music fades in. The elevator dial is moved to the first floor.
(SUZANNE removes her coat and hangs it on the coat rack. HACK removes his shirt and drapes it on the back of the US chair. He gives the bloody towel and sponge to a STAGEHAND who will strike them. The STAGEHAND gives HACK the bandage mitt which he puts on his right hand. The STAGEHAND hangs ALEX's jacket on the coat rack, moves the knife from the table to the bar, and also puts a medical bag, open, on the bar. There is a tube of Neosporin and two vials of blood inside the bag. A STAGEHAND puts two more vials of blood into the sink, and takes his position inside the bar with a pan of blood. TIM and MARY BETH enter and put their coats on the rack, then go to their positions. TIM carries a roll of medical tape and a small pair of scissors. JULIA washes off any blood that has splattered on her hands and face.)

Scene 2

(About two hours later. December 20. Saturday. 1:20 a.m.
(The music fades out as the lights fade up. HACK is now seated at the chair US of the table. He is shirtless, his shirt draped on his chair back; his chest and back are as pasty white as his face and also reveal numerous acne scars. TIM is seated on the chair SR of the table, putting a final strip of medical tape on a mitt-like bandage on HACK's right hand; some blood has seeped onto it at the finger tips. TIM wears a pair of cord pants, a sweat shirt and loafers — clothes hastily thrown on. MARY BETH is seated

on the desk chair. She wears maternity slacks and top, maybe a sweat suit outfit. JULIA is seated on the chair SL of the table; she will seem pensive. SUZANNE is seated on the recliner, swiveled to face onstage, the gun still in her hand. Tim's medical bag and the butcher knife are on the bar.)

TIM. That'll do for now. He really should go to the hospital for a blood transfusion ... and a tetanus shot.

SUZANNE. Why? I didn't think animals could get lockjaw. That's all Hack is — an animal.

HACK. *(Chuckling.)* You'll never change, any of you. You talk about me as if I weren't even here. You treat me worst than an animal, Suzanne. I mean, you talk to animals, don't you?

SUZANNE. Not wild animals. You talk to pets; wild animals — savage ones — you destroy.

MARY BETH. Capital punishment is what you deserve, Hack! There! I said it! I used to campaign against the death penalty, but I've changed my mind. Call me a hypocrite if you want to, but now ...

HACK. *(Cutting in.)* Now that some big, bad murderer has killed someone you know, you want to see him punished, you want justice, you want VENGEANCE! — am I right? You didn't give a shit as long as I stuck to tramps and whores, did you? I'll bet you would have even marched outside the prison for me, holding a picket sign, wouldn't you, Mary Beth? "Save the whales!" "Save the porpoises!" "Save the misunderstood murderers!" They're all the same to you, aren't they? Your "humanitarian" causes? All you have to do is see a protest group march by, and you get in line like a mindless lemming. That's the way you were in school. I'll bet when you were a little girl and played "follow the leader," you never got to be the leader, did you, because all you can do is follow. What's your latest cause. Fetuses? I'll bet now that you're pregnant, you're really big on saving fetuses. Ever get the urge to take a bomb and blow up those motherfuckers who cut the little tadpoles out of women's wombs?

MARY BETH. *(Jumping to her feet; upset.)* Shut up, Hack! Shut

THE REUNION

up! Shut up! Shut up! You're a monster! I hope they strap you in the electric chair and ... and ...

TIM. *(Rising and going to MARY BETH.)* Calm down, Mary Beth. Don't let him get to you. You can't afford to let your blood pressure shoot up. *(He seats her.)* I agree with you — Hack has to pay for his crimes, but I don't think Ohio uses the electric chair, more's the pity.

(He returns to his seat during:)

SUZANNE. Who knows which state will get to do the honors? We're sure Hack has killed people here in Ohio, and Millie and her husband in Chicago, in addition to no telling how many victims in San Francisco, from what Julia told us. What do they do in situations like this? Do the various states' governors get together and draw straws to see who gets to put this sick fuck away? Excuse my language, Mary Beth.

MARY BETH. *(Regaining her composure.)* That's okay, Suzanne. I've heard you say worse.

TIM. And often.

SUZANNE. Watch it, Tim — instead of shooting you a bird, I might just shoot you.

TIM. If you did, it really would be a case of "physician heal thyself."

(He and SUZANNE smile.)

HACK. Listen to yourselves — making jokes about shooting each other. Violence is no big deal when you can laugh about it, is it? Pain can be a lot of fun, and sexy.

MARY BETH. Leave it to you to think of such a thing.

HACK. Oh, it's not just me. Lots of people get off on pain. Have you ever stepped inside a well-stocked porn shop, Mary Beth? Forget I asked — your idea of being sexually adventurous is probably to straddle Alex and fuck him with you on top.

MARY BETH. *(Embarrassed.)* Oh ...

HACK. But I'll bet you know what I'm referring to, don't you, Suzanne? You always were a wild child. Ever try a little S&M? Ever handcuff a guy to the bed and smack him with a belt? Maybe drip hot candle wax on his body? Ever been screwed by a man wearing a leather mask with a zipper for a mouth? *(Angry, SUZANNE clinches her teeth, rises, and crosses to the corner UL, her back to the room. HACK laughs.)* Oh, ho, ho ... What's the matter, Suzanne? Did ol' Hack guess a nasty little secret?... or maybe I got her e-mail address from Julia's computer, hacked into Suzanne's, and found she had put some really disgusting web sites on her "favorites" list.

TIM. Leave her alone!

HACK. Why, Tim! What are you, her knight in shining armor? Are you going to save the innocent damsel, Lady Suzanne, from the horrible dragon? I believe, according to the rules, you're supposed to protect virgins, not sluts.

TIM. I said that's enough!

(He grabs HACK's injured hand and squeezes it. HACK gasps.)

HACK. Ah! That hurts.... Maybe I've been zeroing in on the wrong subject. You like hurting me, Tim?

TIM. *(Releasing his hand.)* No. My goal is to ease pain, not cause it.

HACK. So you say.

JULIA. He doesn't comprehend that, Tim — your desire to help others. Hack is evil, and if he could, he'd spread it like a disease.

(SUZANNE turns back to face into the room.)

HACK. I was wondering when you were going to join the conversation. You give me too much credit, Julia. I think there's a bit of evil in everyone. Some have more than others. I have more than most. The

THE REUNION

shrinks tell us to "get in touch with our inner selves." I got in touch with mine, and look what happened. You should try it sometime. All of you should try it sometime.

(The ELEVATOR MOTOR STARTS. The elevaor will ascend from the first floor to the fourth. The dial will indicate this. TIM rises, puts the tape and scissors into his medical bag on the bar, takes it to the credenza, and sets it down. A beat after he rises, JULIA rises and crosses to SUZANNE.)

JULIA. Why don't you go into the bathroom and pat cold water on your face?
SUZANNE. I think I will. *(Indicating the gun.)* Uh ...
JULIA. I'll hold it for you.
SUZANNE. You sure you won't shoot yourself in the foot?
JULIA. *(Smiles.)* I think I can handle it.

(SUZANNE gives her the gun and EXITS into the bathroom, shutting the door. JULIA crosses to the recliner and sits on its US arm. There is a DING and the elevator doors open. ALEX ENTERS. He wears a sweat shirt, jeans and sneakers. The doors will slide shut behind him.)

TIM. Any problems?
ALEX. No. *(He crosses down to MARY BETH.)* Are you feeling okay, honey? You look a little flushed.
MARY BETH. Hack said some mean things to me.

(ALEX scowls and crosses to SR of HACK.)

ALEX. *(Threateningly.)* You want to repeat them in front of me, Hackett?
MARY BETH. Alex, don't ...
JULIA. His thoughts aren't worth repeating. Let it go, Alex. Did

you...?

ALEX. Yeah. Callie's ... remains ... are at the door to your loading dock. *(He crosses to the sink where he will wash his hands, then dry them on a paper towel.)* Where's Suzanne?

TIM. Bathroom. *(He crosses to ALEX.)* I need to scrub my hands too. I smell like Hack. *(To ALL.)* I told you he'd stink.

(He will wash and dry his hands.)

HACK. I'm offended. I took a long, hot shower just a few hours ago.

JULIA. The trash container is behind the door under the microwave. *(ALEX opens the door and puts the used paper towel into the trash container there. TIM will follow suit. The bathroom door opens. SUZANNE enetrs.)* Feel better?

SUZANNE. Yes.

(HACK rises.)

JULIA. *(Rising and pointing the gun at him.)* Sit down!

HACK. Sorry, but all that running water makes me want to take a piss. You'll have to let me use the facilities, or else clean up the mess.

TIM. *(Crossing to JULIA.)* I'll watch him.

(She gives him the gun.)

HACK. You'll watch me? What's on your mind, Tim? You want to play a little game while we're in there — "I'll show you mine if you show me yours?"

TIM. *(Angry.)* I'm not a homosexual!

HACK. Then I guess all that horseplay in the shower room I remember was just kidding around, huh? You know — snapping a wet towel at the other guys' dicks?

ALEX. Oh, come on...!

THE REUNION

MARY BETH. Tim is engaged to be married!

SUZANNE. He's as straight as an arrow — I can attest to that!

HACK. I'm sure you think so, Suzanne, but, you know, some gates swing both ways.

ALEX. You're full of shit!

TIM. Hey, thanks, guys, but I don't have to prove anything to this lowlife. *(Waving the gun.)* Get in there.

(HACK crosses to the bathroom door. TIM follows. SUZANNE crosses to DL. HACK and TIM exit into the bathroom, closing the door.)

MARY BETH. Why did Hack have to come back!?! We were going to have such a nice reunion, and now he's spoiled it!

ALEX. I guess we should call it off.

MARY BETH. Oh, no ...

ALEX. Can we cancel the arrangements, Julia? And refund everybody's money?

JULIA. Let me think about it.

MARY BETH. I've already bought my dress for the dinner dance. It's the first pretty dress I've got in months. Oh! Suzanne, Alex told me you own a dress shop. I'm sorry I didn't look there.

SUZANNE. It's a fashion shoppe with two p's and an e. You'd be surprised how much that p and e lets me jack up the prices. Don't worry, Mary Beth, we don't carry maternity outfits.

MARY BETH. Oh. Well, I probably couldn't afford one if you did.

SUZANNE. Come by after you've had the baby. That's when you'll really be in the mood for a new dress — one with a waistline. If you find something you like, I'll let you have it at retail — for old times' sake.

MARY BETH. Thank you, Suzanne. For old times' sake ... *(She sniffs.)*

SUZANNE. For God's sake, you're not going to cry, are you!?!

MARY BETH. I can't help it — ever since I got pregnant, my emotions have gone haywire.
ALEX. Tell me about it! Can I get you something, honey? Something to drink?
MARY BETH. A glass of water — tap water will be fine.

(JULIA starts UC.)

ALEX. I'll get it, Julia. *(Facing the cabinets.)* Glasses are...?
JULIA. Your upper right.

(ALEX opens the upper cabinet SL, takes a glass and shuts the door. He will fill it from the faucet at the sink. There is the SOUND of a TOILET FLUSHING. SUZANNE crosses to the chair DS of the table and sits. ALEX takes the water to MARY BETH who sips it. The bathroom door opens HACK enters followed by TIM who holds the gun on him.)

HACK. That was amusing. Dr. Tim was so self-conscious he kept rolling his eyes around in their sockets like mad in an attempt NOT to look at my cock. He couldn't stop himself from catching a glimpse or two, though, could you, Tim?
TIM. My only interest in your penis is to cut if off so you can never spawn another abomination like you.
HACK. Careful, Tim — you're getting into my territory now.
TIM. Sit down.
JULIA. *(Indicating the recliner.)* Over there.
HACK. Whatever you say, beautiful.

(He sits on the recliner.)

JULIA. Tim ... Alex ... *(She indicates the table. ALEX sits on the chair SR, TIM the chair SL. JULIA picks up the butcher knife from the bar and bangs the handle like a gavel.)* The reunion committee is now

THE REUNION 69

in session.

(She lays the knife back down.)

HACK. Oh, God, I can't believe it! I've been admitted into the inner sanctum where the movers and shakers make their momentous decisions! The lowly little peon has finally arrived!

SUZANNE. Tim, do you have any more surgical gauze in your bag? If so, I suggest you use it to bandage up his mouth.

HACK. Why bother, Suzanne? You can just ignore me; you've had years of practice.

JULIA. Thanks to Hack, the committee has some new business we have to attend to. What are we going to do with him?

MARY BETH. Why, we have to call the police. I've been wondering why you didn't call them right away, instead of us.

JULIA. I needed your help.

MARY BETH. For what?

HACK. Isn't it obvious? Moving the girl's body. Am I right, Julia?

JULIA. Yes.

MARY BETH. Why?

JULIA. Mary Beth, I've worked hard to make Jamison Advertising what it is today. If the word got out that a maniac ... *(HACK laughs.)* ... that a maniac killed and dismembered someone in this building, I'd be ruined. Clients tend to shy away from the site of a gristly murder. I'll have to find another apartment in town — I can't live here anymore, not after ... but if I tried to sell the property and relocate the agency, once the word about Callie got out, the stigma would drive the price down to a fraction of what it's worth.

HACK. You always were so practical, Julia.

TIM. So you want the body to be found someplace else.

JULIA. No ... I don't want Callie's body to be found at all.

HACK. Ah... You don't even want to take the chance that it would blight your pristine reputation if it was discovered one of your employees was a murder victim. You prefer to keep your skirts totally clean, am I right?

JULIA. I wouldn't expect you to know what it feels like to build something totally from scratch, Hack — all you know is how to destroy.

SUZANNE. I understand where you're coming from, Julia.

TIM. So the body...?

JULIA. Hack said he disposed of some of his victims by dumping them into the San Francisco Bay. My home on Lake Erie is private; I have a dock and a speed boat.

ALEX. You want to dump the body into the lake?

MARY BETH. But ... that's awful! No one will ever know what happened to her! Her family and friends ... and she should have a funeral ...

HACK. *(In sonorous tones.)* "Dearly beloved ..."

ALEX. Shut the hell up!

MARY BETH. That would be treating the girl like garbage!

JULIA. I know that! And I hate it! I cared a lot for Callie. She was sweet and thoughtful and intelligent.... Her death is such a waste.

HACK. I think I'm going to cry. Boo ... hoo ... hoo ...

(TIM jumps to his feet and jambs the gun against HACK's forehead.)

TIM. I ought to blast you to hell where you belong!

HACK. Then do it. Can you do it, huh, Timmy? Can you? Can you shoot? Here, I'll make it easier for you. *(He takes TIM's wrist and lowers the gun to his mouth.)* Go ahead — shoot into my mouth!

(He takes the gun into his mouth.)

SUZANNE. Tim ...

(TIM stares at HACK a beat, outraged, then, with an exasperated cry, jerks the gun from HACK's mouth, turns, and crosses angrily to

THE REUNION

the sink. He lays the gun on the cutting board SL of the sink, and stands there, his back to the others.)

SUZANNE. *(Rising; to HACK.)* You're lucky you didn't make that offer to me. I would have taken you up on it.

HACK. I think you probably would, Suzanne. You know what they say — that the female is the deadlier of the species. Well ... usually they are ...

(SUZANNE crosses to TIM and talks quietly to him.)

MARY BETH. I don't know how much longer I can stand this!

ALEX. *(Rising.)* Julia, I need to take Mary Beth home.

JULIA. Wait, Alex. We're almost finished ... and I need you.

HACK. *(Rising.)* Don't forget you have to help get rid of the remains. Haven't you figured out by now, Alex, that your contribution to the clique has never been anything more than your brute strength? You're just a dumb jock, and always have been.

ALEX. *(Crossing past JULIA to HACK.)* Listen, you ...

(TIM and SUZANNE turn to watch.)

HACK. *(Cutting in.)* When you got elected student body president I nearly laughed my ass off. You haven't got the BRAINS to lead a cub scout troop! But you were the mighty quarterback on the football team — a star athlete — and that made you Mr. Popularity! ... and it's an unwritten law that the most popular boy in school HAS to be its president, right? Shit! Who composed the little speeches you made in the assemblies, Dr. Tim, there? Or, better yet, Julia? *(To JULIA.)* Was it hard restricting yourself to using words with only two or three syllables so Super-Jock, here, could pronounce them? *(To ALEX.)* I remember hearing you brag about how you were going to really show 'em your stuff when you got to college — that the football scouts were going to discover you for the pros — that some big team would sign you up for millions. What happened, Alex? You didn't become a sports star, you became ... a P.E. teacher! A coach! What a surprise! Actually, it is a surprise — I'm amazed you were able to get a college degree, even one in phys ed. Who did your homework for you, and wrote your class papers? Mary Beth? She's no genius, but she's a damn sight smarter than you are. Is that why you married her, Alex? To do your thinking for you? To sit in the bleachers and cheer for your students at every ball game? To make you feel like a winner? And most important of all, to breed a little Alex, Jr., who might make it to the big leagues, the pros — who might get enough of her smarts to be able to SUCCEED where Daddy fucked-up because he's such a big, dumb FAILURE!?!

(ALEX hits HACK in the jaw, knocking him to the floor. MARY BETH cries out, rising.)

ALEX. I'll kill you, you son-of-a-bitch!!!
MARY BETH. Alex!

(She clutches her stomach and moans. ALEX rushes to her and supports her.)

ALEX. Mary Beth...
JULIA. The baby ...
TIM. *(Crossing with SUZANNE to above the bar.)* Are you having contractions?
MARY BETH. I don't know ... I felt something ...

(HACK gets to his feet US of the recliner. He wipes a smear of blood at his lip with the back of his hand.)

SUZANNE. *(To TIM.)* Maybe you had better check her.

(TIM hurries to his medical bag on the credenza.)

THE REUNION 73

MARY BETH. It's ... it's passed ... I think it's passed ... *(Opening his bag, TIM hesitates.)* Oh, Julia, please — just call the police and have them take him away!

HACK. She can't, you know. If you called the police, I'd eventually be locked up in a maximum security hospital somewhere, but you would all wind up in prison.

ALEX. Why...?

HACK. For aiding and abetting a criminal, dumb-dumb. Didn't you know attempting to dispose of a corpse is a crime? Tampering with evidence, and all that. They might even charge you with being accessories after the fact. Good God, man, haven't you ever watched a cop show on tv? Seen a movie? Read a book? When Julia called you and Tim instead of the police, she knew she'd never be able to turn me in. Didn't you, Julia?

JULIA. Yes.

HACK. It was a question of protecting her career or putting away a serial killer. You know, I'm not terribly surprised at her choice.

MARY BETH. You mean ... you mean we have to let him go?

HACK. Will you, huh, Julia, huh? If I promise to go back to San Francisco and never bother you again, will you believe me?

JULIA. No.

HACK. Smart girl.

MARY BETH. Then what are we going to do?

(JULIA and HACK look at each other a long beat. He smiles.)

JULIA. We have to stop him.

HACK. Ah...

TIM. Julia, I don't think ...

SUZANNE. She's right, Tim. We can't turn him lose on the world. Look what he's done already.

(JULIA stares at HACK another beat, then crosses to the counter,

picks up the butcher block of knives, and crosses back down to SUZANNE. SUZANNE pulls a knife from the block.)

MARY BETH. *(Sinking onto the desk chair.)* Oh, no... *(She starts to cry.)*
HACK. An eye for an eye?
JULIA. Exactly. You have to pay for the suffering you've caused.
HACK. How biblical.

(JULIA crosses to TIM. He hesitates, then takes a knife. JULIA crosses to ALEX. He stares at her a beat.)

JULIA. He said it himself: "An eye for an eye."

(ALEX takes a knife.)

ALEX. *(To MARY BETH.)* You don't have to.

(Suddenly, HACK rushes to the sink and reaches for the gun on the chopping block. SUZANNE beats him there and stabs her knife into the board, stopping him.)

HACK. You can't blame a guy for trying. *(JULIA puts the butcher block on the table, steps to the bar, and picks up the butcher knife there. She crosses above the bar. ALEX and TIM follow her. They surround HACK, JULIA and SUZANNE behind him, ALEX and TIM in front.)* How does it feel to be part of a group? One that will always stick together, through thick and through thin? Till hell freezes over? Can you do it? Can you really do it?

(JULIA stabs HACK in the back. He gasps.)

JULIA. That was for Callie.

HACK. You surprise me, Julia — I thought Suzanne would be the first ... with her masochistic tendencies ...

(SUZANNE stabs him in the back. He brings his hand to his mouth; blood spills between his fingers.)

SUZANNE. That was for Millie.

(TIM stabs him in the stomach.)

TIM. For Randi.

(ALEX stabs him in the stomach.)

ALEX. For her husband and kid.

HACK. *(In gasps.)* You're missing all the fun, Mary Beth.... You know, I was really looking forward to getting together with you. In spite of all my experience, I've never performed a Caesarean ... *(ALEX stabs him again. TIM, JULIA and SUZANNE attack as well. They make vicious, animal noises — grunts — as HACK screams out in pain. MARY BETH, still sobbing, rises, crosses to the table, and takes a knife from the block. She joins the others and begins to stab HACK as well. Blood splatters on all of them. [SEE PRODUCTION NOTES.] HACK screams out:)* At last — I'm one of you!!!

(He sinks to the floor behind the bar, the others sinking with him, still stabbing, their bloody hands and knives rising and falling into view above the bar. Finally, they are still. Blood flows onto the floor at both sides of the bar. Slowly, they rise, one at a time, ALEX helping MARY BETH. They lay their knives in the sink or on the bar.)

MARY BETH. So much blood...

TIM. Ten pints...

ALEX. *(Taking MARY BETH to the desk chair.)* Sit over here, honey. We'll take care of the mess.

MARY BETH. We had to...?

ALEX. We had to.

TIM. We were removing a cancer, Mary Beth. Think of it that way. I do.

(He goes to the sink and washes his hands. JULIA and SUZANNE cross from behind the bar and to SL.)

JULIA. Alex, the office they're painting where you got the tarp for Callie? We'll need more.

ALEX. Yes.

(He goes to the sink and washes his hands. He and TIM will dry their hands on paper towels.)

JULIA. Mary Beth, we'll need your Jeep Cherokee to take the bodies to the lake — his and Callie's — but we can drop you at home on the way. While we're taking care of things in here, why don't you take a shower — we'll all need a shower. Hand out your clothes and I'll put them into the wash; I have a washer and drier in a utility area off the bedroom.

MARY BETH. That sounds so handy. Ours is in the basement. Alex has had to do the laundry for the last couple of months.

ALEX. I'm glad to do it, honey. *(He crosses to the elevator.)* You do as Julia says. *(He pushes the button. The doors slide open. He exits into the elevator.)* Take a nice shower. I'll be right back.

(He pushes the button off SL. The doors close. The ELEVATOR MOTOR STARTS. The elevator will descend to the second floor. The dial will indicate this.)

THE REUNION

TIM. I nicked myself. I'd better put some Neosporin on it. *(Looking down at HACK's body.)* I hope to hell I didn't get any of his blood on the wound.

(He crosses to the credenza, takes a tube of ointment from his medical bag, and applies some to his hand.)

MARY BETH. *(Rising and crossing to JULIA and SUZANNE.)* Do we really have to cancel the reunion? I know it won't be the same now, but ...
JULIA. I don't see why we can't go on with it. Matt Edwards is a priest now. We'll have him say a prayer for our departed classmates.
MARY BETH. That's nice ...

(She crosses to the bathroom and exits inside.)

JULIA. My robe is on the back of the door. You can wear it until your clothes are dry.
MARY BETH. Okay.

(She shuts the door.)

SUZANNE. Matt the cat is a priest? Father Edwards?
JULIA. He sure is.
SUZANNE. Well, I'll be damned! I was thinking of asking the old tomcat over to my place for a drink after the dance — to get reacquainted. Scratch that idea!
TIM. *(Crossing back to SR of the table.)* Maybe you should check the souvenir booklet before the reunion, Suzanne, and see who's married and who's not. That way you won't waste your energy flirting with guys who aren't available.
SUZANNE. Who says married men aren't available?

(The bathroom door opens a crack. MARY BETH, behind it, hands out her clothes.)

MARY BETH. Julia...?

(JULIA takes the clothes. MARY BETH shuts the door.)

SUZANNE. Well, you might as well take this, too. *(She begins to take off her dress.)* God knows I'm not modest, and if I'm going to help you clean up, it'll only get in the way. Shit! I love this dress, and putting it through the washer will ruin it. I guess it can't be helped.
TIM. Take my stuff. *(He starts to undress.)* I've got on silk shorts. Just pretend you're watching me on the basketball court.
SUZANNE. Hot damn! Now, this is what I call getting the reunion off to a good start!

(The lights begin a slow fade.)

TIM. Oh, guess what? Arnie Holt owns a travel agency now. I called him today and talked him into donating a pair of airline tickets to the Bahamas. I figure they'll be our grand door prize.
SUZANNE. Fantastic! Who do I have to screw to win them?

(JULIA, taking SUZANNE's dress, crosses to TIM. He hands her his clothes.)

TIM. I asked old man Barnes, the principal, to be in charge of the drawings.
JULIA. He must be pushing sixty by now.
SUZANNE. Principal Barnes? I'll think about it.

(The lights fade out.)

CURTAIN

THE REUNION

PRODUCTION NOTES

MUSIC: You might wish to play hit songs from ten years ago as pre-show music. As noted in the script, ominous music should be played between scenes.

INTERMISSION: If you wish, you can perform the play without an intermission. If so, go from Act I, Scene 3 into Act I, Scene 1 without a break. Act II, Scene 2 would become Scene 4 in your program, of course.

BLOOD EFFECTS:

CALLIE'S SLIT THROAT — A trick knife that emits blood would be best, but you can create the effect by having HACK hold a small container of stage blood in his hand next to the knife handle, and squirt the blood on CALLIE's neck as the draws the dulled blade across it.

CALLIE'S SEVERED HEAD — The upper kitchen cabinet SL needs a back that can be removed or hinged to swing out of the way. The shelves inside and their contents are slid out of the cabinet from the back, allowing a space that CALLIE can climb a ladder and crawl into. The plywood panel that separates this cabinet from the one-shelf unit over the sink must be removed, and replaced with one that has a semicircle cut from it, creating an arch that fits snugly around CALLIE's neck. As soon as the elevator doors shut on CALLIE's murder, she must add blood flowing from her nostrils and mouth, and smear blood around her neck. She'll climb into the large cabinet and lay her head in the small one. Fit the replacement plywood divider around her neck. When JULIA opens the door to the small cabinet, it will appear that CALLIE's head is inside. Once JULIA closes the door, CALLIE will exit from the back, the solid plywood divider will be put back, as well as the shelves and their contents in the SL unit, and the back panel closed. Thus, when ALEX opens the cabinet door near the end of the play, the cabinet will appear as it did before. The unit will need to constructed as a platform, actually, so that it will support CALLIE's weight.

HACK'S INJURED HAND — Before the scene, set a pan of

stage blood with a sponge in it into the sink. When JULIA mimes jamming HACK's hand into the garbage disposal, HACK will splash the blood on himself and JULIA, then close the sponge inside his fist. After he wraps his hand in a dish towel, he will gradually squeeze more blood from the sponge to soak the towel.

HACK'S SPLIT LIP — When ALEX hits HACK, he falls to the floor behind the recliner, facing upstage. If you apply fresh blood at the tip of the bandage mitt just before the scene, it will still be wet enough so that HACK can smear some from it onto the back of his left hand. When he gets up, he can wipe the back on his hand across his mouth, smearing blood from his hand to his mouth instead of vice-versa, as it will appear.

THE FINAL BLOODBATH — Put two vials of blood with caps into the sink before the final scene. When JULIA and SUZANNE move behind HACK they can remove them, masked by HACK's body, and pour the blood onto their hands and the blades of the knives, then drop the vials back into the sink. When TIM goes to the medical bag when MARY BETH seems ill, he can reach inside and palm two similar vials of blood and hold them against the blade of the knife JULIA gives him. When he and ALEX close in on HACK, their backs to the audience, TIM will pass one vial to ALEX. When they stab HACK, they can uncap the vials and splatter him and their hands and knife blades with the blood. When HACK tries to get the gun on the chopping block, he slips a small piece of blood-soaked sponge beside it into his left hand and palms it. When SUZANNE stabs him in the back, he brings the hand to his mouth, supposedly to catch the blood he's spitting up, but he actually slips the sponge into his mouth and bites it, forcing the blood out of his mouth to spill between his finger. A STAGEHAND will need to sit inside the backless bar before the scene, along with a pan of blood, perhaps the one from the sink. When everyone attacks HACK, the STAGEHAND will fling blood up onto all of them. He will then pour blood onto the floor on both sides of the bar after HACK has fallen and the other rise.

THE REUNION 81

PROPERTY LIST

PRE-SET: ACT I, SCENE 1

Julia's coat - rack
Butcher block w/knives (dulled) - counter
Chopping board - counter
Liquid soap dispenser - counter
Dish towel - counter
Roll of paper towels - counter
Drinking glass - counter
Coffee maker (plugged into outlet) - counter
Microwave - counter
Sugar bowl & creamer - SR cabinet
Food items (stage dressing) - SR cabinet
Plates, bowls, drinking glasses, etc. (stage dressing) - SL cabinet
5 cups & saucers - SL cabinet
1 drinking glass - SL cabinet
Can of coffee w/measuring cup - cabinet over sink
Package of coffee filters - cabinet over sink
Carton of half-and-half - refrigerator
Sara Lee chocolate cake in carton - refrigerator
Foodstuffs (stage dressing) - refrigerator
5 spoons - end drawer under the SL cabinet
5 cloth napkins - next to end drawer under SL cabinet
Trash container - behind door of DL cabinet
Liquid soap in dispenser - by bathroom sink
Computer (plugged into outlet so screen will light) - desk
Computer accessories - desk
Cordless phone - desk
Pad & pencil - desk
Envelope w/checks - desk
2 stacks of paper, paper-clipped, 1 thick, 1 thin - desk drawer

Small Christmas tree - credenza
TV set - (plugged into outlet so screen will light)
TV remote - on cart
Slide projector w/slides in order (plugged into outlet) - on cart

BETWEEN ACT I, SCENES 1 & 2

Strike guests' coats, purses, shopping bag, address book, scrapbook
Return pad & pencil to desk
Strike cups, saucers, spoons, napkins
Replace butcher knife in block
Replace sugar bowl, creamer in SR cabinet
Replace cake in refrigerator
Roll cart with projector against SL wall US of tv
Strike used hand towels by bathroom sink, leaving at least 1 towel
Place Callie's coat on rack
Place Callie's purse w/handkerchief on desk
Place Julia's purse w/lipstick, compact on bar
Turn off coffee maker
Empty coffee, replace pot on coffee maker
Turn switch on florescent light over sink off
Turn switch on floor lamp off

DURING ACT I, SCENE 2

From backstage, prepare the cabinets for Callie

BETWEEN ACT I, SCENES 2 & 3

Wet the butcher knife, place it in sink
Strike Callie's purse from elevator
Place pan of blood & sponge in sink

THE REUNION

AFTER ACT I, SCENE 3

From backstage, replace the shelves in the SL cabinet with their items which should include the cups & saucers used in Act I, Scene 1, washed

BETWEEN ACT II, SCENES 2 & 3

Strike Hack's bloody towel & sponge
Put Hack's shirt on back of US chair
Give Hack bandage mitt with fresh blood on the end
Move knife from table to bar
Set medical bag (open) w/Neosporin, 2 vials of blood inside onto bar
Place Tim's & Mary Beth's coats on rack
Move elevator dial to first floor
Place 2 vials of blood in sink
Place small blood-soaked sponge by chopping block (hidden from view)
Stagehand gets inside bar w/pan of blood

PERSONAL:

ACT I, SCENE 1

Coat, purse, shopping bag w/scrapbook, address book - Mary Beth
Card key - Mary Beth
Hand towels - Julia
Coat - Tim
Beeper - Tim
Coat, purse - Suzanne
Hand towel - Tim
Hand towel - Suzanne
Jacket - Alex

ACT I, SCENE 2

Earrings - Julia
Coat, purse - Suzanne
Knife w/blood - Hack

ACT I, SCENE 3

Coat, purse - Julia
Coat, purse - Suzanne
Hand towel - Suzanne
Coat - Hack

ACT II, SCENE 1

Purse, gun w/blanks - Suzanne

ACT II, SCENE 2

Medical tape, scissors - Tim
Bandage mitt - Hack

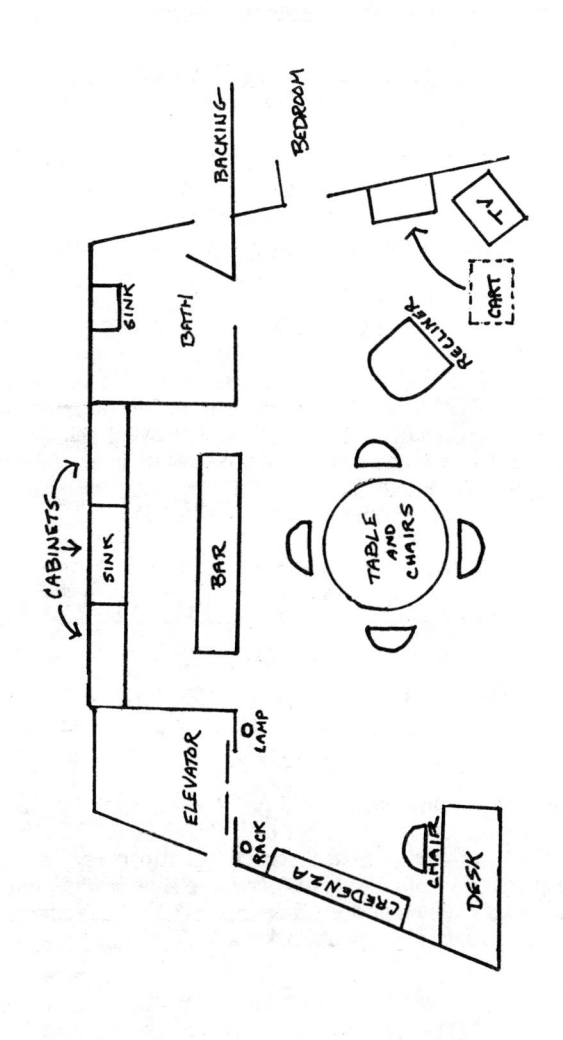

DEATH DEFYING ACTS
David Mamet • Elaine May • Woody Allen

"An elegant diversion."
N.Y. TIMES
"A wealth of laughter."
N.Y. NEWSDAY

This Off-Broadway hit features comedies by three masters of the genre. David Mamet's brilliant twenty-minute play INTERVIEW is a mystifying interrogation of a sleazy lawyer. In HOTLINE, a wildly funny forty-minute piece by Elaine May, a woman caller on a suicide hotline overwhelms a novice counselor. A psychiatrist has discovered that her husband is unfaithful in Woody Allen's hilarious hour-long second act, CENTRAL PARK WEST. 2 m., 3 f. (#6201)

MOON OVER BUFFALO
Ken Ludwig

"Hilarious ... comic invention,
running gags {and] ... absurdity."
N.Y. POST

A theatre in Buffalo in 1953 is the setting for this hilarious backstage farce by the author of LEND ME A TENOR. Carol Burnett and Philip Bosco starred on Broadway as married thespians to whom fate gives one more shot at stardom during a madcap matinee performance of PRIVATE LIVES - or is it CYRANO DE BERGERAC? 4 m., 4 f. (#17)

Samuel French, Inc.
SERVING THE THEATRICAL COMMUNITY SINCE 1830

Grace and Glorie
TOM ZIEGLER

"A sentimental odd-couple crowd pleaser."
THE NEW YORK TIMES

"A slick piece of entertainment."
NEW YORK DAILY NEWS

Estelle Parsons and Lucie Arnaz starred on Broadway in this charmer set in the Blue Ridge Mountains. A feisty 90-year-old cancer patient who has lived her entire life in a remote cabin and a newly transplanted urban hospice volunteer who has lost her young son confound and comfort each other as they share moments of joy and pain. The play is infused with easy humor and spicy exchanges about religion, marriage and other topics related to life's highs and lows. 2 f. (#9944)

Jack and Jill
JANE MARTIN

"An asset by virtue of its human and everyday concerns. ... A worthy play."
VARIETY

This insightful play and excellent source of scene and monologue material by the author of KEELY AND DU and VITAL SIGNS is a series of short scenes that chronicle the birth, life, death and rebirth of a relationship. Jack and Jill climb the hill of romance and marriage, but her constant need to analyze feelings sours their love. They separate for two years and then love rekindles. 1 m., 1 f., extras. (#12902)

Samuel French, Inc.
SERVING THE THEATRICAL COMMUNITY SINCE 1830

The Old Neighborhood
DAVID MAMET

"Heart-piercing ... searing plays....[Mamet's] most
emotionally accessible drama to date."
—*The New York Times*
"This is Mamet unplugged ... a virtuoso of dialogue."
—*New York Daily News*
"Blistering, highly charged theatre."
—*Associated Press*

Bobby Gould returns to Chicago to reconnect with the people and powerful emotions of his past. In three vignettes, he encounters an old buddy, his sister, and a former lover. Hanging over them all is the breakup of community, of family and the Jewish culture that held them together. 3 m., 2 f. (#17710)

Men in Suits:
Three Plays About the Mafia
JASON MILLIGAN

"Hilarious...At turns biting, funny and sad."
—*Fairfield Country Weekly*
"Races by in an ever-changing montage of emotional
loyalty, humor, betrayal and blood.... Fascinating."
—*Connecticut Post*

Each of the three plays in this volume—*ANY FRIEND OF PERCY D'ANGELINO IS A FRIEND OF MINE*: 2 m., 1 f. (#3577); *MEN IN SUITS*: 3 m. (#15292); *FAMILY VALUES*: 6 m., 3 f. (#8597) — is a riveting full-length comic drama. (#21983)

Samuel French, Inc.
SERVING THE THEATRICAL COMMUNITY SINCE 1830